Read and write Greek script

Dennis Couniacis
and Sheila Hunt

For UK order enquiries: please contact
Bookpoint Ltd, 130 Milton Park, Abingdon, Oxon OX14 4SB.
Telephone: +44 (0) 1235 827720. *Fax:* +44 (0) 1235 400454. Lines are open
09.00–17.00, Monday to Saturday, with a 24-hour message answering service.
Details about our titles and how to order are available at www.teachyourself.com

For USA order enquiries: please contact
McGraw-Hill Customer Services, PO Box 545,
Blacklick, OH 43004-0545, USA.
Telephone: 1-800-722-4726. *Fax:* 1-614-755-5645.

For Canada order enquiries: please contact
McGraw-Hill Ryerson Ltd, 300
Water St, Whitby, Ontario L1N 9B6, Canada.
Telephone: 905 430 5000. *Fax:* 905 430 5020.

Long renowned as the authoritative source for self-guided learning – with more
than 50 million copies sold worldwide – the *Teach Yourself* series includes over
500 titles in the fields of languages, crafts, hobbies, business, computing and
education.

British Library Cataloguing in Publication Data: a catalogue record for this title is
available from the British Library.

Library of Congress Catalog Card Number: on file.

First published in UK 2000 as Teach Yourself Beginner's Greek Script by Hodder
Education, part of Hachette UK, 338 Euston Road, London NW1 3BH.

First published in US 2000 by The McGraw-Hill Companies, Inc.

This edition published 2010.

The *Teach Yourself* name is a registered trade mark of Hachette UK.

Copyright © 2000, 2003, 2010 Dennis Couniacis and Sheila Hunt

In UK: All rights reserved. Apart from any permitted use under UK copyright
law, no part of this publication may be reproduced or transmitted in any form or
by any means, electronic or mechanical, including photocopy, recording, or any
information, storage and retrieval system, without permission in writing from the
publisher or under licence from the Copyright Licensing Agency Limited. Further
details of such licences (for reprographic reproduction) may be obtained from the
Copyright Licensing Agency Limited, of Saffron House, 6–10 Kirby Street, London
EC1N 8TS.

In US: All rights reserved. Except as permitted under the United States Copyright
Act of 1976, no part of this publication may be reproduced or distributed in any
form or by any means, or stored in a database or retrieval system, without the
prior written permission of the publisher.

Typeset by MPS Limited, A Macmillan Company.

Printed in Great Britain for Hodder Education, an Hachette UK Company, 338
Euston Road, London NW1 3BH, by CPI Cox & Wyman, Reading, Berkshire,
RG1 8EX.

The publisher has used its best endeavours to ensure that the URLs for external
websites referred to in this book are correct and active at the time of going to
press. However, the publisher and the author have no responsibility for the websites and can make no guarantee that a site will remain live or that the content will
remain relevant, decent or appropriate.

Hachette UK's policy is to use papers that are natural, renewable and recyclable
products and made from wood grown in sustainable forests. The logging and
manufacturing processes are expected to conform to the environmental regulations
of the country of origin.

Impression number 10 9 8 7 6 5 4 3 2 1

Year 2014 2013 2012 2011 2010

Contents

Meet the authors

Like many others before her, Sheila decided that she would like to learn some holiday Greek. Visiting the bookshop, however, she was faced by a daunting array of self-help manuals ranging from basic tourist survival guides to learned tomes full of abstract grammatical terms. All, however, had one thing in common. They did not seem to recognize that decoding the alphabet was so time- and attention-consuming that much of the intended lesson, whether on making simple statements or on a point of grammar was lost. Eventually, having mastered the alphabet in the conventional way, she found a teacher – Dennis – and he confirmed that, as a teacher, he found that Sheila's experience was not unusual, and that if some way could be found to make Greek script easier and faster to conquer, actual language learning could begin much earlier. When the opportunity came to write Read and Write Greek Script, they combined their experiences to produce a book which they hope the student will find turns a chore into something helpful, informative and enjoyable.

Credits

Front cover: © Oxford Illustrators.

Back cover and pack: © Jakub Semeniuk/iStockphoto.com, © Royalty-Free/Corbis, © agencyby/iStockphoto.com, © Andy Cook/iStockphoto.com, © Christopher Ewing/iStockphoto.com, © zebicho - Fotolia.com, © Geoffrey Holman/iStockphoto.com, © Photodisc/Getty Images, © James C. Pruitt/iStockphoto.com, © Mohamed Saber - Fotolia.com

Only got a minute?

If you want to learn Greek, but find the idea of learning the alphabet somewhat daunting, then this is the book for you. Before you tackle even the simplest Greek phrase book, it helps to be able to decipher the script without a second thought, and this book will equip you to do that. However, this could be a rather tedious task, so to make the process of learning easier, and your whole experience more interesting, we give you some insights into Greek life and language, both past and present, whilst teaching you the script.

When you learnt to read English, you probably started with the lower-case letters, with a few capital letters at the beginning of sentences and also for proper names. However, you will have already known the meaning of most of the words which you were reading. Your task this time is different, as the look as well as the meaning of the majority of words will be new, although we try to point out their relationship to familiar words whenever we can.

This different task, therefore, requires a different approach. We start with capital letters, and do not introduce their lower-case equivalents until about halfway through the book. This is because many of the signs you see in Greece or Cyprus are written in capitals, and we think that most learners will want to try out their new skills on a visit to at least one of these two fascinating countries.

There's some more help that we – or rather the Greek language – can give you when learning the Greek alphabet. Unlike English, where the same letter can represent different sounds (think of the 'a' in 'mate', 'mat' and 'malt'), in Greek the same letter, or combination of letters, always represents the same sound.

We trust that this book is merely the first step into what we hope will be a long and fascinating exploration into all things Greek, both ancient and modern.

5 Only got five minutes?

In the first four units of this book, we teach you the entire Greek alphabet as it appears in capital letters, though initially we do not use alphabetical order. Greek alphabetical order is somewhat strange to those familiar with their ABC. For a start, there is no C, as K (kappa) serves equally well for both C and K. The third letter of the Greek alphabet is 'gamma' – the English G, and written Γ in its capital form. There are other surprises too, not least in finding the Greek equivalents for X and Z cropping up quite early in Greek alphabetical order. However, although eventually you will find that knowing these idiosyncrasies – another Greek word which English has adopted – is useful, it is not a priority, and so we have carefully structured our teaching so that you start with either the most familiar or the most easily learnt letters, and then move on to those which may initially appear more difficult or strange. Right from the start we put these letters into words and phrases so that you practise reading, writing and speaking from Unit 1.

Modern Greek has twenty-four letters, almost half of which are the same as they are in English. Once you are comfortable with the individual letters and their associated sounds, we move on to letter combinations and sound blends, giving you plenty of opportunities to practise and revise everything in useful words, phrases and exercises as the book progresses. Having securely established the capital letters, we introduce their lower-case equivalents. Fortunately, most of these resemble their capital-letter counterparts and should not prove too difficult to master. Ancient Greek had a system of accents or 'breathing marks'. Modern Greek has simplified this to a single accent placed above the syllable where the stress, or emphasis, comes. This considerably simplifies the pronunciation of unfamiliar words, and can encourage the learner to practise new skills when, for example, ordering food or drink from a menu.

To reinforce your learning, we include a glossary – a word which, incidentally, comes from the Greek which transliterates as 'glossa' and means language – as well as a mini dictionary covering the words which you will meet in this book. Unit by unit, the glossary reviews most of the new words, along with snippets of what we hope will be interesting information about their derivation, use or association with Greek life.

The story of Greece begins about two thousand years ago, with small groups of nomadic herdsmen, along with their flocks and herds entering the peninsula from the grasslands east of the Caspian Sea. Over succeeding centuries tribe after tribe invaded and spread out into the Aegean Basin, conquering the existing civilization, and assimilating its culture. Gradually they settled, intermarried, and formed small communities presided over by local kings and rulers, which developed into well known city states, of which Athens, Thebes and Sparta are famous examples. Despite warring amongst themselves, the city states flourished, and spread ever further into the Mediterranean lands and also into Asia Minor. If we have whetted your appetite to learn more of the ancient history of Greece, you can turn to our unit at the end of this book, where you will find a more detailed account.

From their language, we know that the people who originally settled in Greece were a branch of the Indo-European speaking peoples. Despite the ability of the early Greeks to conquer and subdue many peoples of the ancient world, their successes do not appear to have included the Ancient Britons, who had to wait for the Romans, Anglo Saxons, Vikings and Normans to enrich and fundamentally develop the English language. However, Greek has proved the perfect medium for transmitting the vocabulary necessary for technical, scientific and mathematical concepts. Although from a modern perspective, Greek has less in common with English than other Indo-European-derived languages such as the Latin based French or Italian, or the Germanic languages such as German or Dutch, nevertheless it has sufficient similarities of grammatical structure and vocabulary to make it relatively straightforward for an enthusiastic learner to make rapid progress.

Although ancient Greek was the forerunner of its modern counterpart, knowledge of one will, unfortunately, be of limited use when learning the other. However, the two scripts are basically the same, and this book, whilst being primarily intended for the modern traveller, could also be the starting point for the student who aspires to study the works of Homer in the original. To cater for as many interests as possible, therefore, throughout the text we have interspersed references to the origins and roots of this fascinating language.

Visitors to Greece or Cyprus are surrounded by reminders of the ancient past, but many travellers may find that their interests lie more in the present. With this in mind, we have assembled some useful and diverse snippets of information to help you find your way around, for instance, or to keep track of time. Each unit is short, giving you the information in a logical and carefully planned way, starting with the letters and sounds resembling their English counterparts, and gradually progressing to the more unfamiliar Greek forms. We have also provided a closing list of suggestions and hints to help you revise and consolidate your knowledge and to give you some ideas for expanding your knowledge. Thus we hope that by the end of this book, we shall have given you both the tools and the enthusiasm to take your study of Greek to the next level, and we wish you every success in your endeavours.

10 Only got ten minutes?

Have you ever had a 'eureka' moment? No doubt you have at some time listened to a symphony, learnt a certain amount of geography, heard of psychology and psychiatry, or used a telephone. It may or may not surprise you to learn that all these words are of Greek origin. If you are coming as a complete beginner to this language, it may also surprise you to discover that the Greek pronunciation of 'eureka' is not the anglicized 'you-reeka' but 'evreka'. However, by the time that you have completed Unit 5 of this book, you will be able to shout 'evreka' like a true-born, native speaker, as well as pronounce more everyday, useful words, phrases and sentences. We also provide snippets of information about Greek life and language, which we hope you will find both interesting and informative.

It is perhaps obvious that 'eureka', an expression made famous by the story of Archimedes and his bath, is a Greek word. To the ancient Greeks it meant 'I have found', and was Archimedes' alleged response to making the discovery that the displacement of water is equal to the apparent loss of weight of an object suspended in it.

The prefix 'sym', or one of its variants 'syn', 'sy', 'syl' or 'sys', and meaning 'with', can be found in modern Greek. Written in capitals, **ΣΥΜ**, it is easily recognizable, since the only symbol new to the learner is **Σ**, 'sigma'. This you may recognize as the summation sign in mathematics, or on a computer spreadsheet. The lower-case version, i.e. **συμ**, is perhaps a little strange at first sight, the initial **σ** being only too easily confused with the cursive form of the English 'o'. This problem should not arise for you, since this book introduces the capital letters first, and you will initially meet their lower-case counterparts in words that have become familiar. You may also have noticed that 'upsilon', **Υ**, has become **υ**. Learning the capital letter first may remind you to pronounce **υ** whenever you meet it as the 'y' in 'sympathy', and not as the English sound found in 'but'. To help you remember μ (called 'me', with a short 'e' as in 'met' in Modern Greek, and not 'mu' as you may know from mathematics), it may be useful to look closely at some packet foods, particularly cereals, where μ combines with the English 'g' forming μg, or microgram – a unit of weight.

Gaia (**ΓΑΙΑ** or **γάια**), 'the earth', has been incorporated into the English language, and is coupled with other Greek words in compounds such as geography, geology or geophysics. Again, there is only one unfamiliar letter, 'gamma', written **Γ** as a capital and **γ** in its lower-case form. 'I' or 'yiota' is pronounced as an English short 'i' unless it is combined with other vowels to make a blend. Unlike English, the lower-case form ι is written without a dot, since it might be construed as a stress mark. When writing words in their lower-case form, Greek has a useful system of marking the emphasized syllable with a stress mark, considerably helping the learner. At one time, written Greek employed a variety of breathing and stress marks. These were used until 1976, when laws were passed making new rules for written Greek which were finally implemented in 1982, to the relief, no doubt, of Greek youngsters as well as struggling foreigners. Since in this book we start with the capital letters, the stress marks will not apply until Unit 6. However, to ensure that you start speaking like a native from Unit 1, we have highlighted the stressed syllable in bold type.

'Psychology' and other words starting 'psych' derive from the Greek 'psyche' or 'soul'. To our eyes, **ΨΥΧΗ**, or **ψύχη** in its lower-case form, looks very strange, although the English form is both a literal translation and transliteration. The first vowel, however, is pronounced as an English short 'i'. In English, too, words starting 'ps' have a silent 'p', whereas in Greek both letters are sounded, and are represented by the Greek letter psi **Ψ** or **ψ**. It is also necessary to remember that **X** or **χ** in lower case is 'chi' with the 'ch' pronounced as in the Scottish 'loch' and is not to be confused with the letter for the English 'x' which is 'ksi', **Ξ** or **ξ** – a distinctive shape, but all those squiggles are tricky to write! Fortunately the first Greek word you will meet in this book is **ΤΑΞΙ** – the Greek for 'taxi' – a ubiquitous sight in Greece, and one which provides a memorable way of fixing **Ξ** in your mind.

Having disposed of symphony, geography, psychology and psychiatry, it is time to turn to the more mundane telephone. When we realize that 'phone' comes directly from the Greek **ΦΩΝΗ** (**φωνέή**) pronounced 'phonee' with a short 'o' sound and the emphasis on the second syllable, and the prefix 'tele' or **THΛΕ** (**τήλε**), and pronounced 'tilly' is from a Greek prefix for far or distant, we can see that many of the everyday English words that we take for granted, owe their origin to Greek. You may have noticed also that the lower-case version of omega (**ω**) bears an unfortunate resemblance to the English 'w'. Once more, this is unlikely to be a problem for you, since you will already be familiar with 'omega' words in capitals. Greek also has another 'o'. It is 'omicron', and is written '**o**'. It is pronounced in the same way as omega, that is with the short 'o' as in 'hot' and not the long sound as in 'moan'. 'Omicron' means 'little o' and 'omega' means 'big o', which explains the prevalence of 'micro' and 'mega' English words.

It is understandable that, with the debt owed by both modern science and mathematics to their roots in ancient and long-vanished cultures, many technical words and ideas should have evolved from these origins, and amongst them Greek symbols and words of Greek derivation are prominent. The Greek symbol for 'p' – **Π** (in lower-case **π**) is probably familiar to anyone with even rudimentary secondary or high-school mathematics, even if the concept is long forgotten or even ill understood at the time of learning. Fortunately, a knowledge of mathematics is not required to make the correct sound when encountering this letter, since it is pronounced in exactly the same way as its English counterpart. What is, perhaps, unexpected is that the letter which we probably pronounced 'pie' is, in fact, 'pi', as in 'pin' without the final 'n'.

Many of our words involving shape are derived from Greek. A pentagon and a hexagon, two-dimensional, straight-sided shapes with five and six sides respectively, come directly from the Greek. Five is 'penday' or 'peday', spelled **ΠΕΝΤΕ** (**πέντε**), and six, or 'exi' is **ΕΞΙ** (**έξι**). Although we usually define these shapes as having five or six sides, the 'gon' part of the word relates to **ΓΩΝΙΑ** (**γωνία**) – pronounced 'gonya' – the Greek word for 'angle' or 'corner'.

These two everyday words illustrate again that, as with our Roman script, some Greek lower-case letters are not just smaller versions of their capital counterparts, but are written differently from their capital form. The English 'N' or 'ni', to give its Greek name, is an easy letter to recognize as a capital, but can confuse the beginner, for obvious reasons, when meeting its lower-case version, i.e. 'ν'. Conversely, the lower-case 'δ', at one time pronounced 'delta,' appears easier to recognize than the strangely shaped 'Δ'. In Modern Greek, however, 'delta' has become 'thelta', and is pronounced like the English 'th' in 'than'. This, in fact, makes the capital letter easier to learn, because it is alien to user of the Roman alphabet, whilst the lower-case version can trip up the unwary.

Greek has another version of 'th'. It is 'theta' – Θ in its capital form, and a smaller edition of the same, i.e. θ, for the lower-case version. You may well have met it in mathematics, where it is often used to refer to an angle.

So far, many of the Greek words in this article have dealt with words of a technical matter or origin. The humble cup of coffee will suffice to introduce 'kappa' – K or κ – and 'fee', written Φ or φ. Thus the Greek καφέ is easily tracked down, but must not be confused with an English café. Incidentally, if you have an interest in art, you may well have come across a concept known as the golden or divine ratio, proportion, number, mean, section or cut, i.e. a dividing of a line into two specific and unequal proportions which are aesthetically pleasing. In mathematical notation, this is often referred to as Φ, the first letter of the name of Phidias, the Greek sculptor who used this ratio in the Parthenon.

By now you have met twenty-one letters, so now there are only three to go, Greek using κ for both k and c, and having no direct equivalent for j. Z or 'zeta' is identical to its Roman equivalent, and in its lower-case form, 'ζ', is easy to recognize as long as one does not confuse it with 's'. The remaining letters are B (β) pronounced 'veeta', and not 'beta', and P (ρ) or 'rho', which, confusingly, is the equivalent of the English R.

You may have noticed that there is no single letter making the sounds of the English B and D. For these basic sounds, you need to write **M** and **Π** – **MΠ** – to make the sound of the English B, and **NT** to make the sound of the English D. Although this may seem strange, if you try sounding **M** and **Π** together, and also **N** and **T**, you will, in fact end up with a close approximation for **B** and **D**.

Having mastered the twenty-four capital letters, you will be ready to blend them. Most blends are easily mastered, with the probable exception of **EY** making EV. We make this process as painless as possible, and with each blend comes the opportunity for an enhanced Greek vocabulary.

There are about fourteen million native Greek speakers, living mainly in, or originating from, Greece and the Greek islands, or the independent areas of Cyprus, and Greek is also a minority language in parts of Italy, Albania and Turkey. Modern Greek descends from Ancient Greek, which in turn derives from the Hellenic strand of supposed proto Indo-European, the forerunner of the vast and diverse family of Indo-European languages. In common with other frequently studied European languages and the 'dead' language of Latin, Greek has similarities in its grammatical structures, as well as some quirks of its own. You will find, for example, that nouns can be masculine, feminine or neuter, they can have different endings according to case, and verb endings vary according to tense and person. By the end of this book, you will be well equipped to begin to unravel the complexities of the Greek language – or just hail a **TAΞI** if you prefer.

Unfortunately, we doubt that this book will furnish you with the insights of an Archimedes, but, nevertheless, we sincerely hope and expect that its study may indeed provide you with many a happy 'eureka' moment.

Prologue

Why did we write this book? After all, as you have probably noticed, there are plenty of books that will teach you all the Greek you need, whether it's to enjoy that idyllic holiday or to meet the challenge of A level. What's new about this book? We'll tell you. This is the only book on the market which is specifically designed to help you decipher the baffling code which at first sight the Greek script appears to be. We know that 'it's all Greek' to you at the beginning and we give you the written script, so that recognizing and pronouncing Greek soon becomes as easy as A, B, C.

'I'm sure 'I'd enjoy learningGreek, if only there was an easy way to learn the alphabet.'

'I'd really like to learn Greek, if only they didn't have that alphabet.'

If you share the views of Mike and Lisa, it's time to let you into a secret. Despite what you may have been told, the Greek alphabet isn't difficult. For a start Greek has only 24 letters, and you've coped with learning 26 at some time in your life, or you would not be able to read this. Of the 24, about a third are written and pronounced in the same way, whether they are Greek or English, so that cuts down the task still further. Even if you manage to learn only one new letter a day, and with our easy methods you'll probably learn faster than that, you will have enough knowledge to pronounce any Greek letter like a native speaker in slightly over two weeks. Greek, you see, has one enormous advantage over English. Every Greek letter, or letter combination, bar one, has only one way of being pronounced. For example, everybody has heard of the Greek drink **ou**zo, pronounced oozo. The good news is that you always pronounce the **ou** like the 'oo' in moon whenever you meet it in a Greek word, unlike English where you come across through, though, bough, cough or enough.

Of course, there is still a certain amount to learn, or we wouldn't have written this book. In each unit we build up your knowledge in small, easily remembered chunks, giving you plenty of practice in pronouncing, reading and writing Greek. You will breeze through situations involving travel, hotels, shops, markets, menus – in fact anywhere that you are likely to meet written Greek. We hope that this book will whet your appetite for this fascinating language, and that you will be keen to go on and learn more!

Insight
If you have studied mathematics at all, you may be familiar with many Greek letters, albeit usually in their lower-case form. However, their mathematical names differ sometimes from the names used in Modern Greek. Where this is so, we have kept to the latter form.

How to use this book

Greek words carry a stress mark which tells you how to pronounce them. The stress mark, however, does not appear until halfway through this book, when we tackle the lower-case letters.

To help your pronunciation we always highlight in **bold** the letter you stress in a word when that word is written in capitals. Where we use transliteration to help you with the pronunciation, we highlight the stress-carrying letter there instead.

That's all there is to it.

Happy learning.

Dennis Couniacis & Sheila Hunt

1

....

ΤΑΞΙ
Taxi

In this unit you will learn
* ***The capital letters A, I, M, N, Ξ, O and T***

Welcome to the Greek alphabet. We have some good news, some bad news and some more good news to give you.

First, some good news. Do these look familiar?

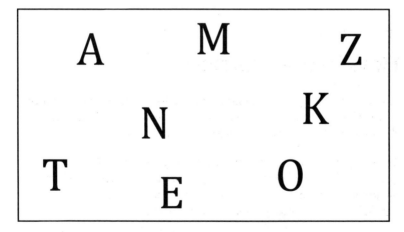

You'll be pleased to know that although they have Greek letter names, these capital letters are pronounced more or less as they are in English. Also, as the Greek alphabet only has 24 and not 26 letters, you already know almost half of them before you start.

It is now time to meat two novice travellers, Mike and Lisa. Together you will learn how to pronounce Greek words, be introduced to some Greek letters (there are seven altogether in this unit) and learn how to combine them to pronounce words you have never seen before!

Now some bad news. In the beginning Greek does have some unfamiliar letters which look … well, Greek to you.

Now some more good news. After you get through the first unit, your ability to read and pronounce Greek will increase very quickly.

To use a phrase book or dictionary efficiently, it is really useful to know Greek alphabetical order. However, you probably didn't start to learn English by reciting your ABC, and we've found the same applies to learning Greek. Later we will give you some tips on alphabetical order, but first things first!

In Greek you will encounter three types of letters: 1) letters which look familiar and you may well know already, 2) letters which look familiar but which don't sound like anything you'd expect, and 3) letters which are totally foreign in appearance (like **Π, Φ,** and **Ω**) and the pronunciation of which you can't even begin to guess.

The reason for all this confusion lies in Greece's history. Greek is a language that has been around for nearly 3,000 years. It has conquered and been conquered. It has borrowed and been borrowed from, and in the process, it has undergone the kind of exciting transformation only a living language is capable of. It is precisely this which makes it both beautiful and infuriating to learn.

Every word you will learn to utter will carry with it the collective sounds of 3,000 years. History will roll off your tongue with every syllable, and, as we all know, history is never straightforward. That's what makes it exciting.

We'll begin our journey into this colourful past with a single word. Appropriately enough, since this is the beginning of our journey (and we kind of just 'stepped' into Greek), we'll begin with the word for 'taxi'. To keep things simple we'll look at the capitals first as it is more likely than not that you'll encounter the word in capitals, anyway.

So step right this way and join Mike as he sticks out a thumb and flags down a **ΤΑΞΙ** (*TAXI*).

Greek pronunciation is pretty much a case of what you see is what you get. That means that each letter has its own individual sound and by stringing the sounds together you can pronounce words you've never seen before.

The **T** in 'taxi' sounds the same as an English *t*.

The **A** sounds like the *a* in 'apple'.

Now here comes the tricky one because the third letter is the 'Ξ'. This is the Greek equivalent of the English '*X*' and the sound it makes is the same as the one found in the word 'tax'.

As a matter of fact the first three letters of the Greek word **TAΞI** are pronounced just like the English word 'tax'. Unlike its English equivalent, though, you will never find the Greek '**X**' (Ξ) at the end of a word.

The final letter in our first word is **I** pronounced like the *i* sound you expect to find in 'tin' or 'pin'.

Putting the entire word together then, this is what we get:

$$T + A + Ξ + I = t + a + ks + i$$

(The Greek word for 'TAXI')

Insight

There is no single Greek letter equivalent for the letter 'j' or its sound. When you need to use it – in some proper names, for instance, we will provide an approximation.

To help you pronounce Greek better there are marks like this: í, over the syllable which is stressed. Unfortunately, though, these are used only for the lower-case letters. We shall look at them later in the book. For now it is sufficient to know that the word **TAΞI** is pronounced TAXI with the emphasis on the last letter.

So if you had to yell for a taxi in Greece you would need, first, to have a good pair of lungs and, second, to stress the second syllable of the word TAXI.

☑ During the reign of Alexander the Great (356–323 BC) Greek was the language of the court and spoken by most of what was then considered the 'civilized' world. Alexander's empire stretched from Greece to India and its creation ushered in the Hellenistic Age, a period of flourishing of the arts and learning that influenced both East and West and outlasted the empire itself.

Practice

Try practising saying TAΞI on your own for a few minutes. Get your tongue used to making the sound. Remember *i* not *ee*, and stress the second syllable.

Now, just like Mike, you are ready to flag down a taxi in tones almost indistinguishable from those of a native speaker!

Exercise

While Mike was learning how to pronounce 'taxi', Lisa came prepared. She already knows letters which are familiar to her.

She knows, for example, that **M** (me) and **N** (nee) are pronounced like ... well, *M* and *N* in English. **O** (omicron) is always pronounced with a short *o* as in 'hot'. Because she believes in being prepared, she is practising writing and pronouncing some basic words. See if you can try your hand at this also. Say each of the words below several times. Remember, understanding Greek script depends very much upon realizing how it all falls together in sentences.

To help you with the exercise we'll tell you that MINI, MONO and NOTA are stressed on the first syllable and MAXI on the second.

MINI (mini) ....

MONO (mono) ....

NOTA (note) ....

MAΞI (maxi) ....

Remember

MINI – This is a Greek mini. To act Greek you have to say *ni* and not *nee*.

MONO – is pronounced like the first two syllables of **mono**tone – also Greek, but that's another story!

NOTA – as in **not a** euro more, **not a** euro less!

MAΞI – English max + i (not *ee*).

Insight

Be careful. As you may know, X does exist in Greek – its name is 'chi' – but the Greek equivalent for the English X is Ξ, although occasionally you may see X on a Greek taxi instead of Ξ, presumably to help (or confuse!) tourists.

It makes sense!

The sounds of the letters you've just learnt are: **A** = a (as in <u>a</u>pple) **M** = m, **N** = n, **O** = o (as in t<u>o</u>p), **I** = i (as in p<u>i</u>n) and **Ξ** = x (as in ta<u>x</u>i). Put the phonetic sound of each letter together and hey presto! You have the word itself.

You've just learnt

A – alpha	**Ξ** – xee
I – yota	**O** – omicron
M – mee	**T** – taf
N – nee	

Total of new letters: 7
... only 17 to go!

A	B	Γ	Δ	E	Z	H	Θ	I	K	Λ	M	N	Ξ	O	Π	P	Σ	T	Y	Φ	X	Ψ	Ω
A								I			M	N	Ξ	O				T					

Test yourself

ΑΒΓΔΕΖΗΘΙΚΛΜΝΞΟΠΡΣΤΥΦΧΨΩ

1 You see a Greek taxi approaching. Which letter is likely to look unfamiliar?

   a T   **b** A   **c** X   **d** I

2 The name the letter in question 1 is

   a kappa   **b** taf   **c** iota   **d** xee

3 You write this letter like this

   a Ξ   **b** T   **c** I   **d** K

4 How does the pronunciation of the word 'TAXI' differ in Greek from its form in English?

5 Using the alphabet printed at the top of this exercise, write all the letters you have learnt so far in alphabetical order.

6 What is the Greek name for each of them?

   You will find the answers in the **key to the exercises** section at the end of the book.

2

ΠΑΝΩ, ΚΑΤΩ
Up, down

In this unit you will learn
- **The capital letters Δ, Ε, Ζ, Κ, Π, Υ *and* Ω**
- **About false friends**
- **Some Greek numbers**

Mike and Lisa are novice travellers. In fact this is their first trip outside their country and they're finding things are a little of a rollercoaster ride as they try to get to grips with Greek script.

Things, however, are not all bad. As Lisa already knows, there are many letters in the Greek alphabet which are almost the same as in English. Our next three letters in the Greek alphabet are 'ups' because you will already recognize them:

K (kappa), **E** (epsilon) and **Z** (zeeta)

Insight

Greek alphabetical order has some surprises. Unlike the
English alphabet, the Greek alphabet does not end in 'z'.

K makes the same sound as the *k* in kettle, **E** makes the same
sound as the *e* in egg and **Z** makes the same sound as the *z* in zoo.

Of course, long before kettles came into vogue and it became
possible to make a cup of tea for one, it is likely that what was
used was a **KAZANI** (kazani = cauldron)!

Insight

Greek manages very well without a 'c', using just kappa,
whereas English complicates matters by using 'c', 'k' or 'ck'.

Other words where **K** is found which you can instantly pronounce
are:

KOMMA (ko-ma)	*comma* (the punctuation mark)
KAKO (ka-ko)	*bad*
KAΔENA (ka-the-na)	*neck chain* (usually gold rather than silver and one which both men and women can wear)

There are a lot more words which you can pronounce the moment you lay eyes on them, but before we get to them, we need to come to grips with a 'down' because this is a purely Greek letter:

Ω

You probably noticed this funny looking letter at the end of ΠΑΝΩ and ΚΑΤΩ. Greek has two different forms of the letter O. One looks just like the English O – O (omicron), and the other looks like Ω, the symbol found in a rather expensive make of watches. It's called omega (with the stress on the middle syllable), but it sounds exactly like an ordinary O as in 'hot' and for all practical purposes you can treat it like one.

Insight

'Omicron' and 'omega' are literally 'little o' and 'big o', but there is no difference to the sound they produce. They are both just 'o'.

So now you can go ahead and try to pronounce this word: ΚΑΝΩ (kano).

Say it aloud a couple of times. It means 'I do / I make'.

Ω is the last letter of the Greek alphabet, so now let's skip back to the beginning, or at least as close to it as we can get in this unit. The fourth letter in the Greek alphabet is Δ (pronounced *thelta*), which looks a little like an Egyptian hieroglyph. The similarity is not entirely coincidental. Many of the single letters of the first non-pictorial alphabet were formed by the Semites of Syria between 1500 and 1000 BC. They borrowed their writing from the Egyptians, though – for the sake of simplicity – they dropped many of the single-word characters employed by Egyptian writing and entirely dismissed the pictorial system used by the Egyptian priests. In 1000 BC the Phoenicians created a new alphabet drawn from the Semitic writing system, which had only 22 letters and was thus both easy to learn and easy to use. The Phoenicians were a seafaring nation and they had many dealings with the Greeks along the Mediterranean coastline. The Greek alphabet, which became the forerunner of all Western alphabets, was borrowed from the Phoenician one, though it was, over time, changed quite considerably.

The letter **Δ** corresponds to the fourth letter in the Phoenician alphabet (*daleth*) and the letter *D* of the Latin alphabet. At one stage, in Greek, **Δ** did indeed have a *D* sound. This changed over the years to a much softer *th* sound such as that encountered in the English word 'the' so that the correct modern pronunciation now is *thelta*. You've already encountered it in **ΚΑΔΕΝΑ** (kathena) and it's used often enough in Greek to be worth its weight in gold!

☑ When the Greeks borrowed Phoenician writing in about the 9th century BC they made many changes to it. The most important one was the direction of writing. Phoenician writing reads from right to left, as do Hebrew and Arabic which it influenced greatly. Initially, ancient Greek writing would go from right to left and then left to right, changing direction alternately from line to line. Gradually, however the left to right direction prevailed in the Greek system and in the Western world.

Practice

At this point stop and practise saying the letter aloud a few times. This will give you a feel for how it sounds when it's put into words.

Now you're ready to go on.

Insight
Remember, **Δ** is thelta, not delta, so is an English 'th' (as in 'that'), not 'd'.

Here are some words where **Δ** is used:

ΕΔΩ (e-th-**o**)	*here*
ΔΥΟ (thi-o)	*two*
ΔΕΞΙΑ (the-xi-**a**)	*right* (as in the direction)
ΔΕΜΑ (th**e**-ma)	*parcel or packet*
ΔΕΚΑ (th**e**-ka)	*ten*
ΔΕΝ (then)	*not*

The best way to practise these words is to say them aloud a few times.

You're not quite out of the woods yet. Before we can go ahead and let you loose to talk to the natives we need to point out one more thing. We promised you some 'downs' and here they are.

False friends

(And we don't mean the ones who are after your money.)

Because of its historically rich background and the great influence which it has had on the formation of the Western alphabet, Greek is full of false friends. These are letters which look familiar, indeed you would swear blind you know what they are, but in reality they sound nothing like what you'd expect. **Υ** (ipsilon) which you met in the word **ΔΥΟ** is one such false friend.

Despite this, what makes Greek easy to learn is the fact that although there are quite a few letters like that, the sound they make is pretty straightforward. **Υ** is just another **I** like you'd expect to find in the middle of words like tin, pin and bin. So, whenever you see it, remember it's just another i.

How much can you remember?

These are all the words which you have met so far. Can you pronounce them all?

NOTA	TAΞI	MINI	MONO	EΔΩ	KANΩ
ΔYO	ΔEΞIA	ΔEMA	KATΩ	MAΞI	ΔEKA
KOMMA	KAKO	KAΔENA			

Try beating Mike at this game by reading all the words aloud in ten seconds.

Exercise 1

Now replace the * with letters to complete the puzzle. You will not need all of the words you've learnt so far.

			E	*	Ω	
		T		E		
		A		K		
*	E	*	I	*		
*		I				
O						

Check in the **Key to the exercises** at the end of the book to see how well you did. If you got most of these, you're on an up which means that you're ready to tackle the last new letter which this unit has to offer.

Π is called pi and it makes the same sound as *p* in pit or pot.

....

Insight

Memories of your school mathematics – fond or otherwise – may encourage you to pronounce π as 'pie', but modern Greeks say 'pi', as in 'pill'.

....

The letter Π is recognizable in the Cyrillic alphabet which is used in some eastern European countries.

Some words which use the letter Π and which you can pronounce are:

ΠΟΤΟ (po-t**o**)	*drink*	
ΠΑΝΩ (p**a**no)	*up*	
ΠΙΝΩ (pino)	*I drink*	
ΠΑΩ (p**a**o)	*I go*	
ΠΑΚΕΤΟ (p**a**k**e**to)	*packet*	

Make it count!

Being in a new country has unsettled Mike a little and he has trouble sleeping. To counter this he has decided to do what his grandma always told him to, which is, to count sheep. Being ambitious Mike has decided to do it in Greek! See if you can go one better by reading the numbers below and then doing the exercise.

1	**ENA** (ena)	10	**ΔEKA** (theka)
2	**ΔYO** (thio)	12	**ΔΩΔEKA** (thotheka)
6	**EΞI** (eksi)	16	**ΔEKAEΞI** (theka-eksi)
7	**EΠTA** (epta)	17	**ΔEKAEΠTA** (theka-epta)
8	**OKTΩ** (okto)	18	**ΔEKAOKTΩ** (theka-okto)
9	**ENNEA** (enea)	19	**ΔEKAENNEA** (theka-enea)

Any questions ; ; ;

The Greek question mark looks like a semi-colon! Therefore in Greek ; = ?

Exercise 2

In the sums below replace the * with the Greek words for the missing numbers.

a	8 + 10 = *	**g**	* × 12 = 12
b	2 + 8 = *	**h**	10 − * = 9
c	12 − 2 = *	**i**	18 − 1 = *
d	18 − 10 = *	**j**	17 + 2 = *
e	8 + * = 10	**k**	8 + 8 = *
f	12 − * = 6	**l**	6 + 1 = *

If you got this far it means that you're now ready to try your hand at identifying useful words and matching them to the pictures in the exercise below. This time we'll be cruel and won't help you at all! Have a go and see how you do. You have already encountered some of the words in this unit and the previous one, but some are totally new to you. That's how much faith we have in the progress you have made.

a

b _____

c

d _____

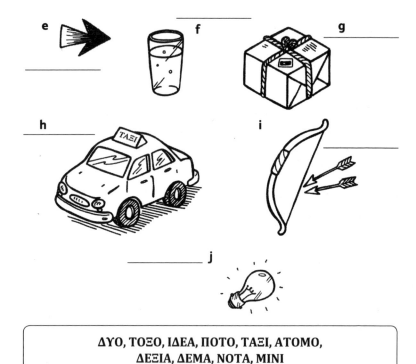

ΔΥΟ, ΤΟΞΟ, ΙΔΕΑ, ΠΟΤΟ, ΤΑΞΙ, ΑΤΟΜΟ, ΔΕΞΙΑ, ΔΕΜΑ, ΝΟΤΑ, ΜΙΝΙ

Match the words in the box with the pictures and write the correct answer in the space provided next to each picture.

Hint

As Sherlock once said, 'once you have ruled out the impossible, whatever remains, however improbable, must be the correct answer'. To match these begin with the ones you know and then try to make an educated guess at the words which are new to you.

So, how did you do?

The pronunciation of the words is:

ΔΕΜΑ (thema) *parcel*
NOTA (nota) *note – musical*
ΔΕΞΙΑ (thexia) *right – the direction*
MINI (mini) *the cult British car*
ΑΤΟΜΟ (atomo) *atom*

ΔΥΟ (thio) *two*
ΤΑΞΙ (taxi) *taxi*
ΤΟΞΟ (toxo) *bow*
ΙΔΕΑ (ithea) *idea*
ΠΟΤΟ *drink*

You've just learnt

Δ – thelta (sounds like *th* in then)
Π – pi (sounds like *p* in pen)
E – epsilon (sounds like *e* in egg)
Y – ipsilon (sounds like *i* in tin)
K – kappa (like *k* in kettle)
Ω – omega (sounds like *o* in top)
Z – zeeta (like *z* in zoo)

Put these with the letters you learnt in Unit 1:

A – alpha	**O** – omicron
M – mi	**T** – taf
N – ni	**I** – yota
Ξ – xi	

You can see that in only two units, you have learnt over half the capital letters in the Greek alphabet.

Total letters: 14
… only 10 letters to go!

A	B	Γ	Δ	E	Z	H	Θ	I	K	Λ	M	N	Ξ	O	Π	P	Σ	T	Y	Φ	X	Ψ	Ω
A			Δ	E	Z			I	K		M	N	Ξ	O	Π			T	Y				Ω

Test yourself

ΑΒΓΔΕΖΗΘΙΚΛΜΝΞΟΠΡΣΤΥΦΧΨΩ

1 In Greek, how many different forms of the letter 'o' are there?

    a 3   **b** 1   **c** 2   **d** 4

2 The Greek letter Δ is pronounced like an English

    a 'd' as in dog   **b** 'th' as in this   **c** 'th' as in think

3 The Greek letter 'Ω' is called

    a omicron   **b** omega   **c** omelette

4 Omicron is the last letter of the Greek alphabet.

    a true   **b** false

5 You may be used to calling Δ 'delta', but the Greeks say '**thelta.**' What English words do you know that are related to ΔΕΚΑ, the Greek for 'ten', or ΔΕΞ ΙΑ, right?

6 Name the two Greek letters which you have met which make the 'I' sound, as in ink.

7 The letters which you now know are Α Μ Ν Ξ Ο Τ Ι Δ Ε Κ Ζ Π Υ Ω. Write them out in alphabetical order.

3

ΕΝΑ ΚΑΦΕ
A coffee

In this unit you will learn
* **The capital letters Γ, Η, Λ, Ρ, Σ and Φ**
* **About Greek café society**

If you've been sightseeing all morning like Mike and Lisa have, it's probably time for a break and maybe even a coffee. Coffee breaks are serious business in Greece so you cannot afford to take this one lightly.

By the time we have finished, you will be able to order at least three varieties of coffee. You will know how to ask for one which is sweet, you'll learn why there's a Greek letter which looks like the gallows out of the old game of 'hangman' and we'll show you a false friend which will blow your socks off!

But let's take things one step at a time. The first letter we tackle in this unit is none other than:

Φ (phi) = fi

Φ makes exactly the same sound as the letter *f* in favourite, five and forever or the combination of letters *ph* which are found in words like phase, physiology and physics. Knowing that, see if you can now work out what the word below is:

ΚΑΦΕ

It's pronounced *kaffe* – but remember, it's 'coffee' and not 'a café'.

☑ Greece has a very advanced notion of the 'café society'. Coffee bars traditionally were the focal points of the community and every neighbourhood had its own. It would be frequented by the people in the area, much as English neighbourhoods have their 'local' pub, and they would then form a very tightly-knit community. The average length of stay in a traditional coffee bar was not expected to be less than four hours with some patrons easily staying twice as long. Time was passed playing backgammon and cards. As you do not need a special licence in order to sell alcohol in Greece virtually every coffee bar sells alcoholic beverages, which range from beer to whisky, and patrons need not restrict themselves only to coffee.

It's not enough however, to just go into a Greek coffee bar and order a coffee.

Before we can satisfactorily explain why, we'll have to throw at least two more letters your way.

The first of these is:

Σ (sigma) = S

This letter makes exactly the same sound as S and you will find it in words such as:

ΣΗΜΑ (sima)	*sign*
ΣΟΚ (sock)	*shock*
ΣΟΦΙΑ (so**fee**a)	*wisdom*

Like most continental languages, Greek tends to borrow English words and transliterate them (as in 'shock'). Unlike in English however there are only 'flat' sounds in Greek, therefore *sh* becomes just another *s* sound, hence the 'sock' pronunciation.

Now unless you're in shock yourself you will have noticed that there is one of those notorious 'false friends' knocking about in one of the words we've just given you.

Take another look at this:
ΣΗΜΑ (sima) = sign.

What looks like the English *H* in Greek, is actually an *i*! It makes exactly the same sound as any other '*i*' you have met so far, so it makes the sound you'd expect to find in tin, pin, or kit. Contrary to popular perception there is a valid reason why there should be so many letters for the sound *i* in Greek. **I** is by far the most frequently used letter in Greek words (much like the letter *e* in English). Inevitably then there are some words which, when pronounced, sound exactly the same (they're homophones, to use a word borrowed from the Greeks) but have different meanings. In order to differentiate between them, it became necessary to be able to write them with a different spelling, hence the different varieties of the letter *i*.

Insight

There are only two capital letters in Greek which are really difficult for writers of English to remember, one of which is H (eta). In time and with practice, it will become automatic, so to speed up the process, try to write and pronounce at least two words containing it every day. (All right, we're all human – replace 'every day' by 'most days'.) You can use the words which you have already met in this book, or any others you can find. See if you can locate H in your phrase book or dictionary.

Back to the task though.

The next vital letter you need to complete your journey towards the promised cup of coffee in this unit is:

$$Λ \text{ (lamda)} = L$$

Λ makes the same sound as the English *L*, so although it looks very different it is actually very easy to use.

Some words which use the letter Λ are:

ΛΑΟΣ (laos)	*people, race*
ΕΛΕΟΣ (eleos)	*mercy*
ΕΛΛΗΝΙΚΟΣ (elinikos)	*Greek* (adj.)
ΛΑΔΙ (lathi)	*oil*
ΠΟΛΥ (poli)	*very*

The last word here is particularly useful as it is also used to refer to a very special type of coffee. Greek coffee is served in a thick, short half-cup (the French call it *demitasse*). It is usually served sweet or very sweet and it is never drunk with milk. If you are tempted to order Greek coffee at all (and you should at least once – it is an experience) be warned. It should be sipped delicately rather than gulped down. The reason for this is that it is brewed from coffee powder which is ground while the coffee beans are still fresh and only then is it lightly roasted. That means that in order for it to be made into coffee it has to be brought to the boil slowly in an old-fashioned, stove-top coffee pot and then poured into a cup. The brewing process produces some very throat-clogging dregs which are poured into the coffee cup along with the coffee and they settle to form a thick sediment at the bottom of the cup. Gulp your coffee instead of sipping it and you will immediately see the wisdom (ΣΟΦΙΑ) of always having a glass of water served with coffee in Greece.

Coffee, sweet coffee!

We're almost there now and we know you can practically smell
the coffee, which is why we've left it until now to introduce the
final letter you will need before you can order your coffee in
Greek. At the beginning of this unit we warned you that it looked
like something you'd expect to see in a game of 'hangman'. If you
played the same type of 'hangman' as we did, then you won't be
surprised to see that the letter is:

Γ

It looks a little like the gallows and it is called gamma. Usually it
can be pronounced as **wh**, except when it is followed by an **i** (any **i**
and in Greek there are six!), in which case, it makes the sound **y**, as
in **y**esterday, **y**ellow and **y**es.

The reason we're learning it now is because the word 'sweet' begins
with it:

ΓΛΥΚΟ (whliko) = sweet

This is a very easy word to remember because the word 'glucose'
actually comes from it.

Other words which use it are:

> **ΓΑΛΑ** (wh-ala) *milk*
> **ΓΙΑΤΙ** (yati) *why*
> **ΓΙΑ** (ya) *for*

In the introduction we mentioned that every Greek letter or letter combination, bar one, has only one way of being pronounced. Well, this is *the* one. **Γ** does some rather funny things to your vocal chords as you will see later on. You've been warned!

☑ Gamma began life looking exactly like the L-plates of learner drivers today. It was stood on its head and reversed by the Semites at around 1500 BC. The Semites made it linear and thought it looked like a throwing stick. They called it *gimel* or *gaml*, meaning 'throwing stick'. The Greeks changed the Semitic name to gamma and, when they began to write from left to right, reversed the direction it was facing so that it looked like a gallows, as it does today.

Exercise 1

And now the crunch. We brought you all this way in the alphabet so you can finally order coffee on your own. There are quite a few ways you can order coffee in Greece, but since we've just learnt about it we'll opt for the cultural experience and go for a Greek one. Remember, let it settle after it arrives and sip it delicately!

In the exercise below you'll have to replace the pictures, symbols and English words with Greek words you have learnt in order to place your order:

A   1×

B   1×

C   1×

Two coffees

There is an anecdotal story which recounts how Greece's Prime Minister during the Second World War, Yannis Metaxas, a man renowned for his quips, was once asked during a pre-election campaign by one of Athens' famous coffee house proprietors, what could possibly be better than a cup of Greek coffee to revitalize a person in the morning. Without batting an eyelid he replied: 'Two coffees'.

Now, in case you feel the same way, we will help you order more than one.

In English, most words which refer to more than one item (plural) simply have -s or -es added to the end. Greek however (you'll be surprised to know), is not that straightforward. Although there are grammatical rules explaining when and how (we won't bother you with those), the reasons for it lie mainly in the phonetics of the language and the need to distinguish between endings which would sound virtually identical in the single and plural form of a word.

Coffee, then, which is **ΚΑΦΕ**, becomes **ΚΑΦΕΔΕΣ**.

✅ The magic word 'please' and its response are not much used in Greece. This is a cultural difference. People in Greece are very casual and laid back when dealing with one another and foreigners. As a result they tend to view excessive politeness as a distancing device and therefore avoid using it. When they say 'please' and 'thank you' they really mean it. It is not just a convention of the language.

Exercise 2

Knowledge almost always comes with some form of responsibility attached. And having now given you the word for 'coffees', we want to see you exercise it by writing out in Greek the English expressions given to you below.

1 Two coffees   **2** Six coffees   **3** Ten coffees

Water!

If you took our advice, waited patiently for your Greek coffee to settle after it was brought to you and then sipped it delicately, the chances are you have enjoyed a fine cultural experience. If, however, you didn't, then we know that you'll need a little more than just the one glass of water which came with your coffee. To prepare you to ask for more, we introduce our final letter in this unit, which, as things go, is probably the worst false friend you're likely to see:

P

We know it looks like a *p*. It isn't!

The letter in Greek is pronounced *rho* and it makes the sound *r* as in river, rover and rivet.

The word water in Greek is: **NEPO**

It is pronounced *nero*, but with a short 'o', and not to be confused with the Roman emperor.

The plural of **NEPO** (just in case) is **NEPA** (nera) and yes, you can ask for two waters in Greek as opposed to two glasses of water.

Insight

We warned you that there were two really confusing letters to learn. Rho (P) is the second one. PHMA looks like an acronym for something pharmaceutical, but is, in fact 'reema' and means 'verb'.

✅ Nine times out of ten a waiter's response to an order is **ΑΜΕΣΩΣ** (amesos) – literally meaning 'immediately'. This is just a turn of phrase. Waiters in Greece are notorious for taking far too many orders at once and keeping customers waiting for some time. The Greeks accept this and use the time to chat and people-watch.

The magic word

Now that you've learnt the letter **P** you can learn the 'magic word' in Greek: **ΠΑΡΑΚΑΛΩ** (parakalo) = please

Exercise 3

Mike and Lisa are unaware of the cultural differences they encounter on their first holiday abroad. They order coffee using 'please' as they would back at home. See if you can order again using the word 'please' this time.

1 Two coffees please   **3** Ten coffees please
2 Six coffees please

The good news now is that with so many of the 'difficult' letters under your belt you're adept enough in Greek to see that words like ΑΓΟΡΑ (pronounced *awhora* – we know it's not *ayora*, don't say we didn't warn you about gamma) must have some connection to agoraphobia (fear of open spaces). ΑΓΟΡΑ, in fact, means 'marketplace' (in ancient Greece this was indeed an open space in the middle of the city. All commercial activity took place there). It also gives you the word: **ΑΓΟΡΑΖΩ** (*awhorazo*) = I buy, or I am buying.

If your taste runs to something stronger than a coffee, you'll have to wait until our next unit where we will join Mike and Lisa as they begin to think about drinks!

You've just learnt

Η – ita	**Λ** – lamda
Φ – phi	**Γ** – gamma
Σ – sigma	**Ρ** – rho

Total new letters: 6
You now know 20 letters altogether. only 4 letters left!

ΑΒΓΔΕΖΗΘΙΚΛΜΝΞΟΠΡΣΤΥΦΧΨΩ
ΑΒΓΔΕΖΗΘΙΚΛΜΝΞΟΠΡΣΤΥΦ Ω

Test yourself

ΑΒΓΔΕΖΗΘΙΚΛΜΝΞΟΠΡΣΤΥΦΧΨΩ

1 Match the Greek expressions to their English equivalents

   1 ΕΝΑ ΝΕΡΟ **2** ΕΞΙ ΚΑΦΕΔΕΣ **3** ΕΠΤΑ ΝΕΡΑ **4** ΕΝΑ ΓΛΥΚΟ ΚΑΦΕ

      a seven waters   **b** a sweet coffee
      c one water   **d** six coffees

2 Put the letters you have learnt in this unit, i.e. Η, Φ, Σ, Λ, Γ and Ρ into alphabetical order.

3 The letters which you now know are Α Μ Ν Ξ Ο Τ Ι Δ Ε Κ Ζ Π Θ Ω Η, Φ, Σ, Λ, Γ and Ρ. Write them in alphabetical order.

4

··

ΕΝΑ ΠΟΤΟ
A drink

In this unit you will learn
- *The capital letters Β, Θ, Χ and Ψ*
- *The letter combinations ΟΥ, ΕΙ, ΑΙ, ΜΠ and ΤΣ*
- *More numbers*

Tired and thirsty from doing the tourist bit, Mike is now ready
for a stiff drink. Greeks share the Mediterranean penchant for
drinking at any time of the day, though never to excess, and in this
unit we shall look at emulating them. Unlike Mike you will get a
lot of practice ordering a vast variety of drinks, learn about a place
where you can order them (more about that in a moment), come
to grips with the final letters of the Greek alphabet and learn about
some combinations of Greek letters which are bound to have you
ordering doubles!

Since you're fresh, strong and eager here's the first one:

OY

This letter combination makes exactly the same sound you'd expect to find in zoo and, handily enough, it is found in the Greek word

OYZO (oozo)

Insight

Be careful! OYZO is an easy word because it is usually familiar to holidaymakers, but it is all too easy to pronounce OY in a less familiar setting as in the English 'JOY' and not as in 'MOON'.

OYZO is made from the pith of grapes after wine makers have finished with them and it is indicative of the native genius for letting few things go to waste. When it is distilled it is a clear, odourless liquid which looks a lot like water. To flavour it, OYZO makers have always used aniseed which gives it its characteristic OYZO taste.

The extract from the aniseed plant (*Pimpinella anisum*) is poisonous in any quantity; however in the minuscule amounts used in OYZO, all it does is impart the characteristic liquorice taste and it also goes cloudy when water is added to it.

Bottled OYZO is sold practically anywhere in Greece, from the local deli to the larger supermarket and everywhere in between. You can drink OYZO in cafés and tavernas. The Greeks, however, never drink without eating and every place that offers drinks is obliged to also offer food in order to attract clientele. Traditionally, small fishing villages and poor neighbourhoods lacked the wealth necessary for setting up and sustaining large restaurants. To meet the need for something small, a new class of drinking establishment arose called OYZEPI (oozeri) – literally a place where one could go to drink OYZO.

Exercise 1

Below we give you a number of other drinks you can buy at an ΟΥΖΕΡΙ along with their pronunciations and English counterparts. See if you can match them by tracing lines joining the Greek word with its pronunciation and its meaning.

1	ΟΥΖΟ	(wh-ala)	*water*
2	ΚΡΑΣΙ	(martini)	*lemonade*
3	ΝΕΡΟ	(ooiski)	*whisky*
4	ΤΕΚΙΛΑ	(portokalatha)	*tequila*
5	ΟΥΙΣΚΙ	(lemonatha)	*milk*
6	ΜΑΡΤΙΝΙ	(nero)	*wine*
7	ΓΑΛΑ	(krasi)	*martini*
8	ΛΕΜΟΝΑΔΑ	(tekila)	*ouzo*
9	ΠΟΡΤΟΚΑΛΑΔΑ	(oozo)	*orangeade*

Insight

Although you may still need to use the English transliteration for help with pronunciation, try to use the Greek version wherever possible. This also goes for using phrase books, the majority of which will have an English pronunciation guide. Trust us; the more you use the Greek version, the sooner it will become automatic.

Never on an empty stomach

Although ΟΥΖΕΡΙ were (and still are) drinking establishments, they also offer food on a very limited basis. The reason why the menu is limited is to be found in the reason ΟΥΖΕΡΙ first came into existence: mainly the lack of money to sustain anything larger. ΟΥΖΕΡΙ today are trendy establishments found all over mainland Greece and the islands. They are there mainly for the locals, though more and more tourists have begun to discover them. Reflecting their origins ΟΥΖΕΡΙ offer two kinds of food: dairy products and seafood.

Try practising saying the words below aloud:

ΜΕΖΕΣ
ΣΑΓΑΝΑΚΙ
ΟΚΤΑΠΟΔΙ
ΚΕΦΤΕΔΑΚΙΑ
ΠΑΤΑΤΕΣ

That's just the kind of fare you will find on the menu of an OUZEPI. Now see how successful you were at deciphering the pronunciation.

ΜΕΖΕΣ (mezes) = a mixed platter which normally contains a couple of meatballs, chips, a sausage and fried goat's cheese.

ΣΑΓΑΝΑΚΙ (sa-wh-anaki) = fried goat's cheese – a delicacy in Greece.

ΟΚΤΑΠΟΔΙ (oktapothi) = octopus, standard seafood in fishing villages. These are marinated to make them tender and shallow fried for a virtually unique taste.

ΚΕΦΤΕΔΑΚΙΑ (keftethakia) = small meatballs
ΠΑΤΑΤΕΣ (patates) = chips

On the bus

Mike has decided to do a little local travelling in order to get to the various eating and drinking places near where he is staying, but before he can do that he has to be able to distinguish one food from another and for that to happen, he has to come to grips with a new letter combination:

ΕΙ

ΕΙ may look hard to make head or tail of, but the sound it makes is simply *i*, just as you'd find in pick, sit and drink. It is found in the word for bus:

ΛΕΩΦΟΡΕΙΟ (leoforio) = bus

Now that you know how to recognize a bus there is nothing to stop you from joining Mike as he sets out for an evening's eating out.

I want

Knowing the menu, being able to pronounce with confidence what is on it, and order a variety of drinks to wash it down with, means that the time has come to learn a brand new letter!

The letter in this case is:

Θ

It is called theta. It makes the sound you'd expect to find in English words like **the**sis, **the**saurus and **the**atre.

Now that you know it you can try using the following word:
ΘΕΛΩ = I want.

> ### Insight
> English has three forms of the present tense. For example, a ccording to the situation, we can say,'I want', 'I am wanting' or 'I do want.' In common with many other languages, Greek has only one form of expression. Also, Greek dispenses with the need to use 'I', 'you', 'we' etc. by changing the ending of the verb instead.

Because Greek verbs have different endings for whoever is performing an action you don't have to worry about learning extra words such as I, you etc.

So:

ΘΕΛΩ	(thelo)	*I want*
ΘΕΛΕΙΣ	(thelis)	*you want*
ΘΕΛΕΙ	(theli)	*he/she/it wants*

ΘΕΛΟΥΜΕ (theloomay) *we want*
ΘΕΛΕΤΕ (theletay) *you want* (plural and formal form)
ΘΕΛΟΥΝΕ (theloonay) *they want*

Insight

As in many languages, Greek has two forms for the second person, or 'you' form, where Modern English has only one. ΘΕΛΕΙΣ is the singular or 'familiar' form, and is mainly used when addressing family members, children, or close friends. ΘΕΛΕΤΕ is the plural version, sometimes known as the 'polite' form, and it is also used in more formal situations.

The good news is that now you can form sentences such as 'I want an ouzo with meze' with the same ease as native speakers, provided of course you have a couple of linking words to hand, otherwise you will be doomed never to get anything **with** something else!

So, final deep breath and here goes.

The two words you need in order to make your culinary experience complete are:

KAI and ME

The first thing you've noticed are the letters **AI**. Before they start to affect your appetite we can tell you that they're easy to pronounce. The letter combination together makes the sound *e* such as you'd find in tender, tepid and trepidation.

That means that the word KAI is pronounced *ke* and it means 'and'.

KAI (ke) = and

The next word is even easier:

ME (mae) = with

The word is pronounced exactly the same as the first syllable of **me**tal.

The good news now is that there is nothing to stop you from ordering a hearty Greek meal.

You now know enough letters and sounds to learn a word which, though basic, can trip up the unwary and lead to all sorts of misunderstanding. The word is NAI, and, unfortunately for native speakers of English, French, German and other languages, means 'Yes.'

$$NAI \text{ (ne)} = yes$$

Exercise 2

In the exercise below the Greek and English sentences have somehow become mixed up. See if you can unravel them by replacing the English words with Greek.

1 ΘΕΛΩ ΕΝΑ ΟΥΖΟ WITH WATER ΚΑΙ ΜΕΖΕ
2 ΘΕΛΟΥΜΕ CHIPS WITH ΚΕΦΤΕΔΑΚΙΑ
3 ΘΕΛΟΥΜΕ ΕΝΑ ΣΑΓΑΝΑΚΙ ΚΑΙ TWO MARTINIS
4 ΔΥΟ ΠΑΤΑΤΕΣ ΚΑΙ ΕΝΑ OCTOPUS PLEASE
5 THREE WHISKIES ΔΥΟ ΠΑΤΑΤΕΣ ΚΑΙ ΕΝΑ ΜΕΖΕ ΠΑΡΑΚΑΛΩ
6 I WANT AN OUZO ME ΝΕΡΟ AND MEZE
7 WE WANT ΠΑΤΑΤΕΣ ΜΕ MEATBALLS
8 WE WANT COOKED GOAT'S CHEESE AND ΔΥΟ MARTINI
9 TWO CHIPS AND ONE ΟΚΤΑΠΟΔΙ ΠΑΡΑΚΑΛΩ
10 ΤΡΙΑ ΟΥΙΣΚΙ TWO CHIPS AND ONE MEZE PLEASE

How about a bottle?

Generally speaking drinks are a lot cheaper in Greece than they are in England, so it would be a good idea to start ordering bottles of everything! Before you can do that, however, we'll have to tell you that there is no individual letter sound for *B* in Greek. Greek gets round the problem by combining two letters to form the sound it needs:

ΜΠ = the English letter *B*

Insight

This is a really weird combination for many learners. However, if you try to pronounce an English M and P simultaneously, you will probably find yourself saying something close to a B.

Now perhaps you can make some sense of the following signs:

ΜΠΑΡ (bar) = *bar*   ΜΠΟΥΚΑΛΙ (bookali) = *bottle*

ΜΠΥΡΑ (bira) = *beer*   ΜΠΟΥΚΑΛΙΑ (bookalia) = *bottles*

In Greek when you want to say 'a bottle of' something, all you need to do is put the words 'one bottle' in front of what you want. 'A bottle of ouzo', for example, becomes ΕΝΑ ΜΠΟΥΚΑΛΙ ΟΥΖΟ.

Exercise 3

Mike is a fast learner. Already he has got into the habit of buying bottles of everything. In the exercise below, see if you can replace the English sentences with Greek ones.

1 Ten bottles of beer, please.
2 Six bottles of wine, please.
3 Two bottles of whisky, please.
4 One bottle of water, please.

Greek uses a few more letter combinations to make single-letter sounds:

ΟΥ – **ΟΥΖΟ**   makes the sound -*oo*
ΕΙ – **ΘΕΛΕΙΣ**   makes the sound -*i*

| ΑΙ – ΚΑΙ | makes the sound -*e* |
| ΤΣ – ΠΙΤΣΑ (*pizza*) | makes the sound -*ts* |

Insight

Many learners find the combination ΕΙ (ee or i depending on the word) sound difficult to remember when they first meet it. However, it is a very common combination in Greek, so you will soon get used to it.

Exercise 4

Entertainment is never to be taken lightly in Greek society. Because of this, a certain specialization has taken place in establishments that provide different types of food and drink. Mike wants to go out to get something to eat, but he has forgotten where he is most likely to find what. See if you can help him by matching the establishment with its identifying food or drink!

ΠΙΤΣΑΡΙΑ	ΟΥΖΟ
ΟΥΖΕΡΙ	ΚΑΦΕΣ
ΚΑΦΕΤΕΡΙΑ	ΠΙΤΣΑ
ΜΠΥΡΑΡΙΑ	ΜΠΥΡΑ

You'll probably notice that coffee now appears as ΚΑΦΕΣ. Greek nouns have a number of forms that necessitate the use of 's' at the end, or conversely the dropping of it. We promised you that this would be fun, so no grammar, which means you'll have to take our word for it! If you get it wrong at this stage, Greeks will understand what you are saying, so no harm done.

A bite to eat

When it comes to eating places, the one most people will have heard of is a taverna. Greek tavernas were the original restaurants. Their menus changed according to what was in season and they served wine drawn directly from a barrel and served in either half litre or litre tin containers – a practice still carried out today. Tellingly, perhaps, a taverna's reputation (and therefore its success) could be made or broken by the quality of its wine rather than its food. Good tavernas would have up to eight different types of wine to draw from. The reason we left it until now, however, is because the tourists' favourite eating place in Greece, when written, displays a 'false friend':

$$TABEPNA = taverna$$
$$\textbf{B} \text{ (beta)} = veeta$$

The letter **B** in Greek, at one stage actually sounded like the English *B*. For a variety of reasons, over the years it was softened from the original beta to veeta and its sound, accordingly, changed from *B* to *V*.

Insight

You may have learnt B (veta) as B (beta), but to the Greeks it just ain't so! It's 'veta', and when found in a word, can be really confusing at first. Fortunately, you will see a TABEPNA on most streets on your Greek holiday, and if you think 'tavern' whenever you see it, you will kill two birds with one stone, and possibly a small OUZO, and master B (veta) and P (rho) in no time.

Other words which use the letter **B** are:

BIBΛIO (vivlio) = book
BAZO (vazo) = vase
BOYTYPO (vootiro) = butter

✔ The letter *B* forms part of the English word 'alphabet'. It was borrowed by the Greeks from the Canaanites around 1000 BC. The Canaanites used a linear form of B adapted from Egyptian hieroglyphics and they called it *beth*, literally meaning 'house'. At that time it stood for a stylized picture of a house. The Greeks changed *beth* to *beta* and from there it entered, unchanged, into the Latin alphabet and then the English.

Pay up!

Before the euro (ΕΥΡΩ – pronounced *evro*: see Unit 5), the Greek currency was the drachma. Although you no longer have to use the drachma while in Greece, it would be a good idea to learn how to say it because it gives us the opportunity to tackle the last one of those 'false friends':

$$\mathbf{X} = \text{hee}$$

While it looks exactly like the English *X* this Greek letter is actually an *H*! It makes exactly the kind of sound you'd find in words like Himalaya, hibiscus and hibernation.

It is also found in the word ΔΡΑΧΜΗ (pronounced *thrahmee*) – the drachma.

Insight

The Greek X approximates to the English H, but is probably closer to the Scottish or German CH as in Loch. Don't confuse it, though, with Ξ, the Greek form of the English X.

You already have 'yes' (ΝΑΙ), and now we can give you 'no'. It is ΟΧΙ (ochi) – unfamiliar, perhaps, but not confusing.

More numbers

2	ΔΥΟ	1000	ΧΙΛΙΑ
3	ΤΡΕΙΣ	2000	ΔΥΟ ΧΙΛΙΑΔΕΣ
100	ΕΚΑΤΟ		

Exercise 5

In the exercise below match the prices Mike has to pay with the price tags:

ΔΥΟ ΧΙΛΙΑΔΕΣ ΕΥΡΩ	
(thio hiliathes evro)	€1000
ΕΞΙ ΧΙΛΙΑΔΕΣ ΕΥΡΩ	
(exi hiliathes evro)	€10 000
ΔΕΚΑ ΧΙΛΙΑΔΕΣ ΕΥΡΩ	
(theka hiliathes evro)	€3000
ΕΚΑΤΟ ΧΙΛΙΑΔΕΣ ΕΥΡΩ	
(ekato hiliathes evro)	€2000
ΧΙΛΙΑ ΕΥΡΩ	
(hilia evro)	€6000
ΤΡΕΙΣ ΧΙΛΙΑΔΕΣ ΕΥΡΩ	
(tris hiliathes evro)	€100 000

Something fishy

With this letter you will have learnt the whole Greek alphabet:

$$\mathbf{Ψ} = psi$$

This letter makes exactly the kind of sound you'd expect to find in English words like harpsichord and **Pepsi**.

Greek words which use this letter include:

ΨΑΡΙ (psari)		*fish*
ΨΩΜΙ (psomi)		*bread*
ΨΩΝΙΖΩ (psonizo)		*I buy*

Insight

As in many languages, Greek only has one form of the present tense, when English has 'I buy' or 'I am buying'.

In a word

Greek society and culture is quite literal. Often occupations and jobs are made of compound words which describe exactly what goes on. So, a baker for example would be a 'breadmaker', while a fish-seller would be ... a fish-seller!

The Greek word for 'I sell' is: ΠΟΥΛΩ (poulo). This can be slightly (but only slightly) modified when combined with other words.

Exercise 6

Match the product with the place that sells it.

ΨΑΡΙ (psari) = fish   ΦΡΟΥΤΟΠΩΛΕΙΟ
ΦΡΟΥΤΑ (froota) = fruit   ΤΥΡΟΠΩΛΕΙΟ
ΤΥΡΙ (tiri) = cheese   ΓΑΛΑΚΤΟΠΩΛΕΙΟ
ΓΑΛΑ (wh-ala) = milk   ΨΑΡΟΠΩΛΕΙΟ

More good news is that now, armed with the entire Greek alphabet as we are, there is nothing to stop us going shopping!

Insight

You may like to impress your friends by writing in Greek on the computer. First you need to set the computer up to write in the Greek language. This is not difficult, but the process varies according to the operating system which you have. Most of the English letters will give you their Greek equivalents automatically, but here is a list of those which don't.

Θ = U   Ξ = J   Ψ = C   Ω = V

Your computer may be different, though. Try checking this by writing the entire alphabet in Greek capital letters.

You've just learnt

ΟΥ	ou – *oo* as in **zoo**
ΕΙ	epsilon yota – *i* as in p**i**t
Θ	theta – *th* as in **th**istle
ΑΙ	alpha yota – *e* as in **e**lephant
ΜΠ	mi pi – *b* as in **b**eer
ΤΣ	taf sigma – *ts* as in le**ts**
Β	veeta – *v* as in **v**ase
Χ	hee – *h* as in **h**en
Ψ	psi – *psi* as in Pe**psi**

CONGRATULATIONS!
You now know all the letters of the Greek alphabet!

Α Β Γ Δ Ε Ζ Η Θ Ι Κ Λ Μ Ν Ξ Ο Π Ρ Σ Τ Υ Φ Χ Ψ Ω
Α Β Γ Δ Ε Ζ Η Θ Ι Κ Λ Μ Ν Ξ Ο Π Ρ Σ Τ Υ Φ Χ Ψ Ω

....

Test yourself

Look back over the words you have met so far, and try to pronounce them without looking at the English transliteration. You can use this to check yourself afterwards.

1 Write these lists of letters in alphabetical order.
  i Δ Κ Α Χ Ζ   **iii** Ξ Θ Ο Ν Β
  ii Ψ Ω Φ Π Μ   **iv** Λ Γ Ι Υ Κ

2 Write in Greek.
  i tavern   **iv** fruit
  ii book   **v** bus
  iii bread and fish

5

ΩΡΑ ΓΙΑ ΨΩΝΙΑ
Time for shopping

In this unit you will learn
- *About shopping in Greece*
- *The letter combinations* AY, EY, OI *and* NT

OK! We know that the unit heading here is hard. Nevertheless we are so confident there is nothing you cannot deal with that we are prepared to take you shopping! The word for 'I shop' or 'I am shopping' in Greek is:

ΨΩΝΙΖΩ = psonizo

And the word for the things you buy, unsurprisingly, is:

ΨΩΝΙΑ = psonia

Before we take you shopping however we will throw one more new word at you:

ΜΑΓΑΖΙ (ma-wh-azi) – shop

Insight
Many everyday words in Greek are not that easy for English speakers to remember. Sometimes a mental picture can help. Imagine a girl called Pauline Sonia, P. Sonia for short,

spending recklessly on shopping. Now run the two words together: Psonia the 'aristocrat' of shopping – Princess Sonia spending recklessly on shopping. Now run the two words together (ΨΩΝΙΑ) and Bob's your uncle (or should we make that ΜΠΟΜΠ instead?). Also, if you have a smattering or more of French, you may have noticed a resemblance between 'magasin' – the French for shop, and ΜΑΓΑΖΙ.

Exercise 1

Mike, who is self-catering, needs to buy some food. He has a complete list of things to buy. Unfortunately his list is in English. Perhaps you could help him by matching up the English on his list with the Greek equivalent.

Bread	ΠΟΡΤΟΚΑΛΑΔΑ
Cheese	ΛΑΔΙ
Beer	ΖΑΧΑΡΗ
Coffee	ΤΥΡΙ
Sugar	ΟΥΙΣΚΙ
Retsina	ΚΑΦΕΣ
Milk	ΨΩΜΙ
Oil (to cook with)	ΜΠΥΡΑ
Whisky	ΓΑΛΑ
Orangeade	ΡΕΤΣΙΝΑ

Exercise 2

Now Mike faces another problem. He has to work out where he can buy the items he needs. Once again he has to rely on your help to guide him. See if you can link the Greek items on the left with the places where they could be found in the box.

1 ΠΟΡΤΟΚΑΛΑΔΑ

2 ΛΑΔΙ

3 ΖΑΧΑΡΗ

4 ΤΥΡΙ

5 ΟΥΙΣΚΙ

6 ΚΑΦΕΣ

7 ΨΩΜΙ

8 ΜΠΥΡΑ

9 ΓΑΛΑ

10 ΡΕΤΣΙΝΑ

| ΣΟΥΠΕΡΜΑΡΚΕΤ |
| ΤΥΡΟΠΩΛΕΙΟ |
| ΓΑΛΑΚΤΟΠΩΛΕΙΟ |

Exercise 3

While shopping for the items on his list Mike has met Lisa, who is also on a self-catering holiday. They have struck up a friendship and he is now planning to take her out. The problem is that he cannot remember where they can be expected to serve what. See if you can help him by matching up the food and drink on the left with the appropriate establishment on the right.

1 ΚΑΦΕΣ   ΟΥΖΕΡΙ

2 ΠΟΡΤΟΚΑΛΑΔΑ

3 ΜΕΖΕΣ   ΤΑΒΕΡΝΑ

4 ΟΥΖΟ

5 ΚΡΑΣΙ   ΚΑΦΕΤΕΡΙΑ

6 ΜΠΥΡΑ

7 ΠΙΤΣΑ

8 ΠΑΤΑΤΕΣ

9 ΣΑΓΑΝΑΚΙ

10 ΚΕΦΤΕΔΑΚΙΑ

ΜΠΥΡΑΡΙΑ

ΠΙΤΣΑΡΙΑ

✅ We mentioned in Unit 3 that Greek has given us the word 'agoraphobia' (fear of open spaces). The original market place where shopping of all kinds took place in ancient Greece was an open space called Agora (ΑΓΟΡΑ). Open-air markets are a weekly feature of Greek urban life. While traditionally you find reasonably priced fresh produce at Greenmarkets, these days you can also buy cheap watches, videos and CDs!

Haggling is a feature of buying that is associated more closely with life on the Greek islands (a remnant of their barter economy) than any market place on the Greek mainland. You are not traditionally expected to haggle when you are buying gifts. However, certain tourist spots, like Corfu and Rhodes, pander to this by artificially inflating their prices. The best way to decide whether you can haggle at a place or not is to shop around and compare prices, like you would at home.

Exercise 4

Mike has discovered that drinks in Greece are cheaper than at home. He has invited Lisa to visit him in his flat and, being the perfect host, he needs to have a drink or two to offer her. He has splashed out on some drinks which are in a jumble below. Work out which drinks Mike bought. If you are right the letters going down the bottle will tell you which one he did not buy because he didn't know the word for it!

		K			-	Σ	I
		N			P	O	
-	A	P		-	I	N	I
O	Y	-		-	K	-	
T	E	-		-	Λ	A	
-	E	M	O	-	A	-	-
		Γ		-	A		

ΚΡΑΣΙ, ΓΑΛΑ, ΛΕΜΟΝΑΔΑ, ΜΑΡΤΙΝΙ, ΟΥΙΣΚΙ, ΤΕΚΙΛΑ, ΝΕΡΟ

Manners please!

Now that we have learnt about culture differences, like saying
'please', we're going to cover the word for manners, or we would
cover the word for manners if there were an exact Greek word
for it! We know what you must be thinking. The Greek word that
is used to mean 'manners' is ΤΡΟΠΟΙ (tropi) = 'manners', 'method',
or 'way'. Instantly, by the definition, you notice that it is not an
exact equivalent. You are right. To narrow down the meaning a
little more, in Greek, you have to say ΤΡΟΠΟΙ ΣΥΜΠΕΡΙΦΟΡΑΣ
(tropi siberiforas) = 'means' or 'manner of behaving'. This isn't
because Greeks have no manners; on the contrary, it is, simply,
a point of cultural distinction. In ancient Greece everyone was
expected to behave themselves. Therefore everyone behaved within

the social norm, and their means or manner of behaviour – ΤΡΟΠΟΙ ΣΥΜΠΕΡΙΦΟΡΑΣ – were equally acceptable. Those few, however, who stood out from the pack by their truly polished politeness and good manners were considered to be ΕΥΓΕΝΕΙΣ (evyenis) meaning 'noble'. Because of this, the word also became synonymous with good and better behaved, and those who were noble were said to be possessed of a certain ennobling quality, called ΕΥΓΕΝΕΙΑ (evyenia) = literally meaning 'nobility'. Hence, today someone who is polite is said to possess ΕΥΓΕΝΕΙΑ (evyenia). Therefore to be ΕΥΓΕΝΙΚΟΣ (evyenikos) is to be polite!

Apart from the fact that the word has lent itself to English in words like **eu**logy and **eu**genics it also gives us the opportunity to explore one more letter combination: **ΕΥ**. The two letters together either make the sound *ev* (as in **ev**olution) or *ef* (as in l**ef**t) depending on what other letter follows in the word.

Other Greek words which use the **ΕΥ** combination are:

ΕΥΧΑΡΙΣΤΩ (ef**h**aristo)	*thank you*
ΕΥΚΟΛΟ (ef**k**olo)	*easy*
ΔΕΥΤΕΡΑ (thef**t**era)	*Monday*

One more thing we must mention here is the use of **ΟΙ**. This is the last *i* you will have to learn in Greek and to all intents and purposes it should be treated as just an ordinary *i* as in king.

Insight
EY and OI are probably the most 'foreign' combinations of letters that an English speaker has to learn. However, if you have previously studied another language, however briefly, you will know that there are quirks and pitfalls in all of them. The good news is that every Greek word follows the rules.

Exercise 5

Mike's problems are far from over. As this is Lisa's first visit to his apartment, he wants to impress her. He has found out that she is a vegetarian. Deciding to play it safe he is going to make an omelette. He knows roughly what he will put in it and he has a list in English, but after only one week in Greece his Greek is still not good enough to do the shopping. See if you can help him by matching the ingredients on his list with the Greek produce.

ΑΥΓΑ	(av-wha)	*bread*
ΓΑΛΑ	(wh-ala)	*tomatoes*
ΛΑΔΙ	(lathi)	*cheese*
ΤΥΡΙ	(tiri)	*salt*
ΒΟΥΤΥΡΟ	(vootiro)	*eggs*
ΨΩΜΙ	(psomi)	*oil*
ΑΛΑΤΙ	(alati)	*butter*
ΠΙΠΕΡΙ	(piperi)	*milk*
ΝΤΟΜΑΤΕΣ	(domates)	*pepper*

NOTE: Just as the Greek letters ΜΠ gave us the English *B* sound, ΝΤ gives us the sound *D*. We will get a chance to practise this combination in the next couple of units.

☑ One of the most common complaints tourists have about Greek food is the temperature it is served at. Hot food, when it comes, is rather tepid. The reason for this is that Greece is a hot country and food is traditionally served lukewarm or tepid rather than hot. This is a minor cultural difference, but, if you like your food served piping hot, it is worth bearing in mind.

Insight

Although it can be tedious learning the alphabet, it really is a useful skill when it comes to looking up words in a dictionary or phrase book. However, it can seem quite daunting, so it's easier to break it down into sections. Can you recite the first five letters now? If you can manage that fairly easily, try tagging Z on to the end. Now try putting together Z, H and Θ. (They rhyme, so make an easy trio.) Next, try reciting this far at odd moments, and when you are confident, add on I. After Θ, come five letters, i.e. I, K, Λ, M and N in the same order as they are in English. Now try to finish the alphabet

More letter combinations

To make an omelette ΟΜΕΛΕΤΑ (omeleta), naturally, you need to break some eggs and in order to do so, you must first be able to say the word so you can buy them.

Eggs is one of those funny words in Greek which depends upon a letter combination. This time it is: **ΑΥ** (pronounced *av* as in **ca**vern).

Depending upon which letter comes after it **ΑΥ** can sometimes make the sound *af* (just like in **af**ter) rather than *av* but we'll cover these as and when we get to them.

Exercise 6

Travel does not always broaden the mind. Sometimes it just helps to confuse one nation's flag with another. In the exercise that follows there are the flags of six nations. See if you can match the Greek names with their English equivalent.

(United States of)
America

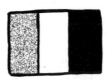
Italy

Greece

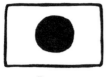

| Japan | Korea | Australia |

ΑΜΕΡΙΚΗ ΙΤΑΛΙΑ ΕΛΛΑΔΑ ΙΑΠΩΝΙΑ ΚΟΡΕΑ ΑΥΣΤΡΑΛΙΑ

Lisa's visit to Mike's holiday apartment has gone like a dream. The omelette he made was edible, the Greek salad he prepared was good and they both had a few drinks. As a matter of fact they are so excited by the discovery that this is the other's first trip abroad that they have decided to meet the following day to tackle the lower-case letters of the Greek alphabet together. We shall, of course, join them.

You've just learnt

AY	– *av* or *af*	**OI**	– *i*
EY	– *ev* or *ef*	**NT**	– *d*

To consolidate what you have learnt after you have completed 'Test Yourself, we suggest that you read through the Glossary on p. 108 as for as the end of Unit 5. All the words that you have learnt so far are there along with snippets of information with which to impress your friends.

....

Test yourself

ΑΒΓΔΕΖΗΘΙΚΛΜΝΞΟΠΡΣΤΥΦΧΨΩ

Fill in the gaps below. Try to do as many as you can without using the alphabet printed above.

1

i A B Γ - E Z H - I K Λ M N - O Π P Σ T - Φ X - Ω

ii A B - Δ E - - Θ I K Λ M - - - Π P Σ T - - X Ψ Ω

iii A - Γ Δ - - - - I K Λ M N Ξ O - - - T - - - - -

Now is a good time to take stock of what you have already learnt. Try to fill in the missing letters, by referring back to the first five units if necessary, before checking the answers.

Unit 1

1 M - - O   **2** T A - I   **3** N - T -   **4** - A Ξ -

Unit 2

1 Δ E - I -   **2** K A - E - A   **3** - Y O   **4** - - Ξ O

Unit 3

1 K A - E   **2** Γ A - A   **3** N E - O   **4** Π - P A K - Λ-

Unit 4

1 O - Z O   **2** Λ E M - N A - A   **3** Λ E - Φ O P E - O   **4** M - A P

Unit 5

1 T - P -   **2** - T - M A T - -   **3** - Ω M -   **4** E - Λ A - A

6

ΨΩΝΙΑ
Shopping

In this unit you will learn
- *Lower-case letters*

Well, here we are, with all the capitals of the alphabet completed and about to rush into the world of the lower-case letters. These will be easier because there are stress marks to help you pronounce the words. As before, there's good news and there's ... even better news. The good news is that Greek does not have joined-up writing, therefore the letters you'll learn stay pretty much the same when they're written by hand. The even better news is that many letters remain the same as they were in their capital form. They're just written smaller! This explains why capitals and lower-case letters are usually referred to in Greek as 'big' and 'small' letters: ΜΕΓΑΛΑ (mewhala) and ΜΙΚΡΑ (mikra).

Insight
Also, as you already know, 'big o' – , omega, and 'little o' – O, omicron.

Exercise 1

However, before we rush headlong into the lower-case letters, we'll just make one final foray into the world of the capitals. Cover up the English list, and see if you can unmask the mystery fictional detectives by saying their equivalent Greek names aloud.

Draw a line connecting the correct answers.

POIROT   ΣΕΡΛΟΚ ΧΟΛΜΣ
SHERLOCK HOLMES   ΠΟΥΑΡΟ
PHILIP MARLOW   ΕΠΙΘΕΩΡΗΤΗΣ ΜΟΡΣ
ELLIOT NES   ΜΑΓΚΝΟΥΜ
MAGNUM   ΦΙΛΙΠΠΟΣ ΜΑΡΛΟΟΥ
INSPECTOR MORSE   ΕΛΙΟΤ ΝΕΣ

Sleuths

We promised you some practice with the combination of Greek
letters that give us the sound *D* and we're just about to deliver.
All of the fictional personalities in Exercise 1, to a greater or
lesser extent, are detectives. The Greek word for 'detective' has
been taken directly from the English and it's used to mean both a
detective (as in the police rank) and a private investigator.

Below we give you the word in capitals. First practise saying it
aloud a few times, just so you can get your tongue round it.
Next, see if you can rewrite it in the space provided using only
lower-case letters. Check with the list of lower-case letters in this
unit if you are not sure.

ΝΤΕΝΤΕΚΤΙΒ

- - - - - - - - - -

A	B	Γ	Δ	E	Z	H	Θ	I	K	Λ	M	N	Ξ	O	Π	P	Σ	T	Y	Φ	X	Ψ	Ω
α	β	γ	δ	ε	ζ	η	θ	ι	κ	λ	μ	ν	ξ	o	π	ρ	σ	τ	υ	φ	χ	ψ	ω

Exercise 2

Now that you're so good at this, see if you can match the Greek
names on the left with the English ones on the right.

Ντόναλντ Ντάκ	Davy Crocket
ΝΤΕΙΜΠΙΝΤ ΚΡΟΚΕΤ	Diana Ross
ΝΤΑΙΑΝΑ ΡΟΣ	Danny de Vito
Ντάνι ντε Βίτο	Donald Duck

Insight

Although you may still need to use the English transliteration for help with pronunciation, try to use the Greek version wherever possible. This also goes for using phrase books, the majority of which will have an English pronunciation guide. Trust us; the more you use the Greek version, the sooner it will become automatic.

Exercise 3

Mike has a problem. He likes Lisa and would like to impress her even more. After she left his apartment he stayed up half the night going through his language guide books trying to learn the names of the places he would like to take her to. What he has discovered is that a lot of the signs in shops are in lower-case letters and these look very different from their capital counterparts! See if you can help him by matching the capitals with their lower-case letters in the list below.

ΠΙΤΣΑΡΙΑ	Ουζερί
ΟΥΖΕΡΙ	Μπυραρία
ΚΑΦΕΤΕΡΙΑ	Πιτσαρία
ΜΠΥΡΑΡΙΑ	Καφετερία

Here's one you'd never guess

Because of its Ancient Greek roots, modern Greek positively bristles with words loaded with poetic imagery. Take the one below for example:

ΟΠΩΡΟΠΩΛΕΙΟ (oporopolio) = fruit shop

The basis of this one comes from the word ΟΠΩΡΑ (opora) meaning 'produce from trees', which originally would have been the only kind of fresh produce available to buy. While no one calls it ΟΠΩΡΟΠΩΛΕΙΟ any more, the signs outside fruit shops still serve as a reminder of days when greenhouses and international trade did not exist.

See if you can now substitute lower-case letters for each upper-case one of the word:

ΟΠΩΡΟΠΩΛΕΙΟ

Lower-case letters

Although you've already met some lower-case letters and now know just how easy it is to leap from the capitals to them, it might help if, at this stage, we started from the very beginning:

A α – alpha   *α*

B β – vita   *β*

Γ γ – gamma   *γ*

Δ δ – thelta   *δ*

E ε – epsilon   *ε*

Z ζ – zita   *ζ*

H η – ita   *η*

Θ θ – thita   *θ*

Next to each of these we have included the handwritten version which is different for some. The reason handwriting is slightly different from what you will see on shop signs and windows has more to do with the human personality than grammar, so it's sufficient to say that it differs and leave it at that. Now that you're ready we'll tackle the rest of the lower-case letters:

Ι ι – yota	ι	P ρ – rho	ρ
Κ κ – kappa	κ	Σ σ – sigma	σ
Λ λ – lamtha	λ	T τ – taf	τ
M μ – mi	μ	Υ υ – ipsilon	υ
N ν – ni	ν	Φ φ – fi	φ
Ξ ξ – ksi	ξ	X χ – hee	χ
0 o – omikron	o	Ψ ψ – psi	ψ
Π π – pi	π	Ω ω – omega	ω

Insight

As you can see, just over half of the lower-case letters closely resemble their capital counterparts. These are β, ε, θ, κ, ι, λ, o, π, ρ, τ, φ, χ, ψ.

Remember, though, that 'ι' has no dot on the top.

☑ Modern Greek is derived from ancient Greek. At some point in its past, however, it went in two different directions and was transformed. The main reason for this change was the power wielded by the Greek Orthodox Church in the old Byzantine Empire. Byzantium outlived the Holy Roman Empire by a thousand years before succumbing to the Ottomans. Religion figured very prominently in Byzantine life and the language of the Church was a highly ornate, slightly convoluted form of Greek which was not really spoken by ordinary men and women. Because it was spoken by the Church a certain, not entirely unwarranted perhaps, degree of prestige was associated with it. As a result shop signs used the more ornate way of describing what they sold, a practice which is reflected to this day!

Insight

Other lower-case letters which are easy to recognize for writers of the Roman alphabet are α, δ and υ. That only leaves eight to learn.

Exercise 4

Mike is finding himself getting in deeper and deeper problems. As he looks at all the places he wants to take Lisa to, he realizes that he can understand some of them but others do not seem to bear much resemblance to anything he knows. See if you can help him untangle the mess he is in by matching the place with its English definition and what it sells or what services it provides! To help you in the task we have provided a glossary at the end of the book. To make things harder though we used only lower-case letters. See how you do. Use the list at the end of the unit to guide you.

ΧΡΥΣΟΧΟΕΙΟ	bakery	ΚΑΦΕ
ΞΕΝΟΔΟΧΕΙΟ	hotel	ΦΙΛΜ
ΑΡΤΟΠΩΛΕΙΟ	jeweller's	ΧΟΡΟΣ
ΖΑΧΑΡΟΠΛΑΣΤΕΙΟ	café	ΦΑΓΗΤΟ
ΚΑΦΕΤΕΡΙΑ	cinema	ΨΩΜΙ
ΕΣΤΙΑΤΟΡΙΟ	restaurant	ΧΡΥΣΟΣ
ΚΙΝΗΜΑΤΟΓΡΑΦΟΣ	pâtisserie	ΓΛΥΚΑ
ΝΤΙΣΚΟΤΕΚ	disco	ΔΩΜΑΤΙΟ
ΦΑΡΜΑΚΕΙΟ	chemist's	ΑΣΠΙΡΙΝΗ
ΤΑΧΥΔΡΟΜΕΙΟ	post office	ΓΡΑΜΜΑΤΟΣΗΜΑ

Exercise 5

Look at the following names of some Greek newspapers. First say
the name of each newspaper aloud. Then, in the space provided,
replace the capitals with the lower-case letters:

ΑΠΟΓΕΥΜΑΤΙΝΗ,   ΑΚΡΟΠΟΛΗ,   ΜΕΣΗΜΒΡΙΝΗ,

_____   _____   _____

ΚΗΡΥΚΑΣ,   ΕΘΝΙΚΗ,   ΠΕΛΟΠΟΝΝΗΣΟΣ,

_____   _____   _____

How did you do?

Check your answers in the Key to the exercises and if you've scored
less than 5/6 look at the capitals and lower-case letters again!
Circle the ones which you've got wrong and practise writing them
a few times. Recognition comes only with repetition!

Insight

Probably the only two letters which should carry a health
and safety warning are η (Η) and ν (Ν). Remember 'η' is not
an English 'n', but ita, which is an 'i' sound, and 'ν', or ni
which, for obvious reasons, is almost bound to catch you out
at first. Fortunately, as it crops up in many common words,
it does get easier to remember to pronounce it as 'n'
and not 'v'.

Exercise 6

In the exercise below you need to identify which price tag belongs
to which group of words. Unfortunately they are all jumbled up
and the words are in lower-case letters!

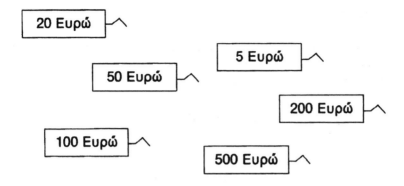

είκοσι ευρώ, εκατό ευρώ, πενήντα ευρώ, διακόσια ευρώ, πέντε ευρώ, πεντακόσια ευρώ.

One extra letter

The number of lower-case letters in the Greek alphabet is, funnily enough, one more than the capitals! This is because of the letter Σ (sigma). In its capital form, sigma presents no problem, but when we go to the lower-case letter, we have to be more careful. A different form of sigma is needed at the beginning and in the middle of a word from the one needed at the end. The sigma which is used at the end of a Greek word is, to all intents and purposes, identical to the English -ς. The sigma used at the beginning and in the middle is simply -σ.

So, ΓΛΥΚΟΣ 'sweet', which is what you want the coffee you're ordering to be, becomes in lower-case γλυκός.

In a long word like 'locomotive', for example, the letter -s occurs twice. We give you the word in capitals and ask you to write it in lower-case letters:

ΣΙΔΗΡΟΔΡΟΜΟΣ (sithirothromos)

☑ Many of the words we use in the English language have been passed on to us by the Greeks, though we don't necessarily use them in the same context. The Greek word for 'newspaper', for example, is ΕΦΗΜΕΡΙΔΑ (efimeritha). This has given rise to the word 'ephemeral' – which is what news is by nature!

Literally speaking

A lot of the modern Greek words came about as exact descriptions of what they are.

ΣΙΔΗΡΟΣ (sithiros) means 'iron' and ΔΡΟΜΟΣ (thromos) means 'road'. So, ΣΙΔΗΡΟΔΡΟΜΟΣ stands for both the railway network (literally, iron road) and the trains which run on it. Of course, the more modern word for 'train' is ΤΡΑΙΝΟ (treno).

Insight

Try writing your name and that of your friends using Greek letters. You will have to approximate some sounds, for example, using Σ for Sh, ΤΣ for Ch and ΤΖ for J, about which we shall learn more in Unit 8.

Exercise 7

In the next exercise Mike and Lisa face a problem. They want to buy a ticket for a ferry crossing. Unfortunately the book they have uses numerals to number the words written in capital letters, lower-case Greek letters to number their definitions in English, and capital Greek letters to number the words written in lower-case Greek letters! Our two friends are totally confused. See if you can help them by matching the number with its equivalent letter in both Greek and English to arrive at the lower-case form and definition of the word. One has been done for you as an example:

Example: 11 ΑΕΡΟΠΛΑΝΟ   μ *aeroplane*   Μ αεροπλάνο

1 ΣΙΔΗΡΟΔΡΟΜΟΣ	α	*train*	Α	τρένο
2 ΛΕΩΦΟΡΕΙΟ	ε	*helicopter*	Β	λεωφορείο
3 ΑΥΤΟΚΙΝΗΤΟ	δ	*ferry*	Ε	ελικόπτερο
4 ΦΕΡΙΜΠΟΤ	ζ	*coach*	Δ	φεριμπότ
5 ΕΛΙΚΟΠΤΕΡΟ	θ	*cable car*	Η	φορτηγό
6 ΠΟΥΛΜΑΝ	β	*bus*	Κ	τανξ
7 ΦΟΡΤΗΓΟ	ι	*submarine*	Γ	αυτοκίνητο
8 ΤΕΛΕΦΕΡΙΚ	γ	*car*	Θ	τελεφερίκ
9 ΥΠΟΒΡΥΧΙΟ	κ	*tank*	Ζ	πούλμαν
10 ΤΑΝΞ	η	*truck*	Ι	υποβρύχιο
11 ΑΕΡΟΠΛΑΝΟ	λ	*taxi*	Μ	αεροπλάνο
12 ΤΑΞΙ	μ	*aeroplane*	Λ	ταξί

Insight

Many Greek words are very literal. The Greek word for railroad for example: ΣΙΔΗΡΟΔΡΟΜΟΣ means 'iron road'. It also stands for the train itself, or 'locomotive'.

Exercise 8

This morning Mike found that he needed a few odds and ends, so he has spent the last half hour dashing from shop to shop, before meeting up with Lisa at their favourite café. Unfortunately his bag has become mixed up with those of other shoppers. Mike bought something at each of the following shops and also at a fruit and vegetable stall. Can you guess which bag is his?

ΖΑΧΑΡΟΠΛΑΣΤΕΙΟ
ΑΡΤΟΠΩΛΕΙΟ
ΓΑΛΑΚΤΟΠΩΛΕΙΟ
ΒΙΒΛΙΟΠΩΛΕΙΟ
ΤΑΧΥΔΡΟΜΕΙΟ

You have met most of these words before. However, so as not to make it too easy, we have thrown in a few new ones, but you won't have any problems with them.

Bag 1	Bag 2	Bag 3	Bag 4	Bag 5
ψωμί	γάλα	γλυκό	ένα πορτοκάλι	ψωμί
πέντε	μήλα	ψωμί	γραμματόσημα	τυρί
ντομάτες				
μπουκάλι	βιβλίο	κρασί	τυρί	ένα γλυκό
κρασί				
φέτα	γραμματόσημα	τυρί	ουίσκι	καρπούζι
γιαούρτι	σοκολάτα	βούτυρο	δύο βιβλία	βούτυρο
τυρί	ψωμί	γάλα	γιαούρτι	γάλα

μήλα	*apples*	**σοκολάτα**	*chocolate*
γιαούρτι	*yoghurt*	**καρπούζι**	*water melon*
μπισκότα	*biscuits*	**βούτυρο**	*butter*
λεμόνια	*lemons*	**πορτοκάλι**	*orange*

χρυσοχοείο	*jeweller's*	φαγητό	*food*
αρτοπωλείο	*bakery*	ψωμί	*bread*
ντισκοτέκ	*disco*	χρυσός	*gold*
ταχυδρομείο	*post office*	γλυκά	*sweets*
φαρμακείο	*chemist's*	δωμάτιο	*room*
κινηματογράφος	*cinema*	φίλμ	*movie/film*
εστιατόριο	*restaurant*	καφέ	*coffee*
ξενοδοχείο	*hotel*	ασπιρίνη	*aspirin*
ζαχαροπλαστείο	*pâtisserie*	γραμματόσημα	*stamps*
καφετερία	*cafeteria*	χορός	*dance*

Α	Β	Γ	Δ	Ε	Ζ	Η	Θ	Ι	Κ	Λ	Μ	Ν	Ξ	Ο	Π	Ρ	Σ	Τ	Υ	Φ	Χ	Ψ	Ω
α	β	γ	δ	ε	ζ	η	θ	ι	κ	λ	μ	ν	ξ	ο	π	ρ	σ	τ	υ	φ	χ	ψ	ω

....

Test yourself

You have already met all these words, so look back through the first six units if you need help.

1 Write these words in their lower-case form.

ΜΑΞΙ   ΜΙΝΙ   ΚΟΜΜΑ   ΠΑΝΩ   ΔΕΝ   ΛΑΔΙ   ΓΑΛΑ   ΚΡΑΣΙ   ΕΥΡΩ
ΨΑΡΙ   ΣΟΥΠΕΡΜΑΡΚΕΤ   ΒΟΥΤΥΡΟ   ΦΑΡΜΑΚΕΙΟ   ΣΟΚΟΛΑΤΑ
ΓΡΑΜΜΑΤΟΣΗΜΑ

2 Write these words in capital letters.

αλάτι   αυγά   ρετσίνα   πίτσα   μπισκότα   εστιατόριο   ξενοδοχείο
ψωμί   ζάχαρη   φρούτα   χίλια   βιβλίο   θέλω   μαρτίνι
οκταπόδι

7

....

Τρώμε έξω
Eating out

In this unit you will learn
- ***About eating in Greece***

Eating out is a national pastime in Greece. As in most Mediterranean countries, people in Greece use eating out as a means of getting together with friends and family. Not surprisingly, prices are cheaper, though nowhere as cheap as they used to be, and there is a large variety of restaurants catering to demand.

Below is a menu from one of them. It is written in a combination of lower-case and capitals, and also in English. The printer was very good at languages but terrible with numbers. He left out half the prices in Greek and half the ones in English. See if you can choose a meal from the list below and then work out how much it will cost you.

MENOY

Γεμιστά	€4,50
Πατάτες φούρνου	
Πατάτες τηγανητές	€2,40
Παστίτσιο	€3,70
Μακαρονάδα Μπολονέζα	€4,40
Μπριζόλα χοιρινή	

Μπριζόλα μοσχαρίσια	€6,40
Κεφτέδες	
Σαλάτα χωριάτικη	
Σαλάτα μαρουύλι	

MENU

Stuffed tomatoes	
Potatoes cooked in the oven	€2,70
Chips	
Pastitsio	
Spaghetti Bolognese	
Pork chop	€5,40
Beef chop	
Meatballs	€3,50
Greek salad	€2,90
Lettuce salad	€0,90

☑ In Greek the word for 'potatoes' and 'chips' is the same: πατάτες. Potatoes feature quite a lot in Greek cooking. To differentiate between all the different ways of cooking them, Greeks usually describe how they're cooked beside the name. 'Chips', for example, become πατάτες τηγανητές, literally 'fried potatoes'; you can also have πατάτες γιαχνί (steamed potatoes), πατάτες φούρνου (potatoes cooked in the oven), πατάτες βραστές (boiled potatoes) and so on. Because 'fried potatoes' is a long way to say 'chips', Greeks usually call them either πατάτες on its own or πατατάκια (little potatoes) which leaves no doubt whatsoever as to the meaning.

Fast food (Φαστ φουντ)

Greece is not immune to modern-day pressures, however, and fast food restaurants are popular with young and old alike for the speed and convenience they provide. Below we have a number of fast food items you may recognize.

Exercise 1

See if you can match the Greek with their English counterparts:

ΧΑΜΠΟΥΡΚΕΡ, ΣΑΝΤΟΥΙΤΣ, ΣΑΛΑΤΑ, ΠΑΤΑΤΕΣ, ΣΩΣ, ΚΕΤΣΑΠ, ΜΟΥΣΤΑΡΔΑ, ΜΠΕΙΚΟΝ

sauce, salad, mustard, chips, bacon, sandwich, ketchup, hamburger

How did you do? Check in the Key to the exercises to see how many you got right.

Now see if you can provide the lower-case equivalent for each one.

Exercise 2

Goody's is a fast food chain in Greece, in the same vein as McDonald's. It aims to provide as healthy a meal as possible. Mike and Lisa decide to try it out. Unfortunately, they've mixed up their translations so they are no longer sure which description fits which choice. See if you can help them by translating the English back into Greek. To help you we have provided some Greek words below.

χάμπουρκερ, σως, ντομάτες, μαρούλι, κρεμμύδι, ψωμάκι, τσίλι, πίκλες, μουστάρδα, μπέικον

Translations:

Burger, bread roll, mustard, pickle, sauce

Burger, bread roll, bacon, chilli, sauce, onion, lettuce, tomatoes

Exercise 3

If you have matched the translations correctly you should be able to provide the Greek capitals for the following words:

1 Bread roll
2 Sauce

3 Lettuce
4 Bacon
5 Tomato

Exercise 4

Goody's try to provide a lot more than just hamburgers in their menu. Look at the pictures and descriptions of the choices below.

1

ΚΟΤΟΠΟΥΛΟ GOODY'S

Φιλετάκια από στήθος κοτόπουλου, τριμμένο καρότο, σως μουστάρδας, μαρούλι, ντομάτα

2

TEXAS DOUBLE

Ψωμάκι με νιφάδες σταριού, μπιφτέκια, μπέικον, σως barbeque, τηγανητές πατάτες, κρεμμύδι, μαρούλι, ντομάτα

3

ΛΟΥΚΑΝΙΚΟ

Λουκάνικο, τηγανητές πατάτες, σως μουστάρδας, τριμμένο καρότο, μαρούλι

4
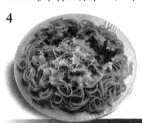

GOODISSIMO ΛΕΥΚΟ

Ζυμαρικό τύπου Linguini, σάλτσα λευκή, μανιτάρια, μπέικον, τριμμένο τυρί (παρμεζάνα και σκληρό τυρί)

5

ΜΠΙΦΤΕΚΙ ΜΕ ΤΥΡΙ

Μπιφτέκια, τυρί, σως Goody's, τηγανητές πατάτες, τριμμένο καρότο

6

GOODISSIMO ΚΟΚΚΙΝΟ

Ζυμαρικό τύπου Linguini, κόκκινη σάλτσα, τριμμένο τυρί (παρμεζάνα και σκληρό τυρί)

Now find in which of the choices on the menu the following ingredients appear:

1 Κοτόπουλο (chicken)
2 Καρότο (carrot)
3 Μπέικον
4 Τυρί

Exercise 5

Goody's also do a traditional fish supper! Look at the description below and list all the ingredients in capitals.

FISH FILET

Φιλέτα ψαριού, σως tartar, τριμμένο καρότο, τηγανητές πατάτες, αγγούρι, μαρούλι

✓ Traditionally, Greek cuisine was dictated to a large extent by the necessities of a mountain-dwelling community. As a result meat does not feature very heavily in it and there are a lot of vegetarian dishes. However, as mountain-dwelling existence is, by definition, harsh, calorie-rich olive oil was used a lot. It continues to play an important role in the Greek diet today, though the rigours of modern Greek life are somewhat less than those of its ancient past.

Exercise 6

After a hearty meal at Goody's you should treat yourself to an ice cream (ΠΑΓΩΤΟ).

There are three to choose from. Decide which type of ice cream has the ingredients given on above.

ΠΑΓΩΤΟ GOODY'S

Κρέμα με Cookies, Σοκολάτα με Choc Chips,
Κρέμα με Καραμελωμένα Καρύδια

1 Κούκις
2 Caramelized walnuts
3 Chocolate

Test yourself

Now's the time to really test yourself. Either get this right or risk feeling hungry.

1 Without looking back through the unit see if you can remember what the following words mean: Καρότο, πατατάκια, μπέικον, σως, τυρί,

2 Write the following words in capitals: χάμπουρκερ, σως, ντομάτες, μαρούλι, κρεμμύδι, ψωμάκι, τσίλι, πίκλες, μουστάρδα, μπέικον

3 Now write the following words in lower-case letters: ΧΑΜΠΟΥΡΚΕΡ, ΣΑΝΤΟΥΙΤΣ, ΣΑΛΑΤΑ, ΠΑΤΑΤΕΣ, ΣΩΣ, ΚΕΤΣΑΠ, ΜΟΥΣΤΑΡΔΑ, ΜΠΕΙΚΟΝ

4 What's the Greek word for bacon?

5 What's the Greek word for chicken?

8

Στο μουσείο
At the museum

In this unit you will learn
- *The days of the week*
- *The letter combination* TZ

You cannot visit Greece without going to at least one museum. Mike and Lisa decided to visit one in Athens. The problem was agreeing on the day to visit it. Lisa thought that Tuesday would be a great day to go but Mike wanted to explore the countryside on a bus on Tuesday. The museum would not be open on the first working day of the week and it would be closed for renovation for the two days prior to Friday, after which it would be open as normal. Mike was suffering from sunburn after the weekend and needed a day to recover and Lisa was adamant that Friday should be set aside for island hopping.

Exercise 1

Below are the days of the week in capitals and underneath are spaces for you to write in the lower-case letters. Work out, from the text above, which days of the week are available for Mike and Lisa to go to the museum. Write your answers in lower-case letters.

Monday	Tuesday	Wednesday	Thursday
ΔΕΥΤΕΡΑ	ΤΡΙΤΗ	ΤΕΤΑΡΤΗ	ΠΕΜΠΤΗ
_____	_____	_____	_____

Friday	Saturday	Sunday
ΠΑΡΑΣΚΕΥΗ	ΣΑΒΒΑΤΟ	ΚΥΡΙΑΚΗ
_____	_____	_____

☑ The Acropolis is by no means unique to Athens. Every Greek city state had one. Traditionally it was a complex of buildings at the highest point of the city. Its position was selected so as to be easily defended and present natural obstacles to any attacker. In the days of ancient Greece the fear of raids from pirates as well as rival city states was very real. If a city state saw itself losing a battle, it would withdraw its army and citizens to the acropolis, surrendering the rest of the city to the invader. Acropolis is a compound word formed from two words, ΑΚΡΗ meaning 'edge' and ΠΟΛΗ meaning 'city'. Acropolis therefore meant literally the edge of the city, or its highest point.

Insight

The need to have an Acropolis, in the ancient world, was a matter of survival. As a result it also became part of the city's social and ritualistic life with the temples of their gods being situated there.

Exercise 2

In order to make the most of their time in Greece, Mike and Lisa decide to rent some transport. The guidebook they're using, however, has got wet and some of the letters have faded. They have another guidebook but everything is in lower-case letters. The problem is that this guidebook offers no definitions.

Perhaps you can help them by filling in the missing capitals from the words written in lower-case.

1 ΣΙ_ΗΡΟ__ΟΜΟΣ = *train*	1 σιδηρόδρομος
2 ΛΕΩΦΟΡ___ = *bus*	2 λεωφορείο
3 Α___ΚΙ_ΗΤΟ = *car*	3 αυτοκ;ίνητο
4 ΠΟ_ΛΜ_Ν = *coach*	4 πούλμαν
5 ΦΩΡΤΗ__ = *truck*	5 φορτηγό
6 ΠΟΔΗ__ΤΟ = *bicycle*	6 ποδήλατο
7 Β_ΣΠΑ = *scooter*	7 βέσπα
8 ΤΖ_Π = *Jeep*	8 Τζιπ

One more letter combination

As we have already stated, there is no single letter which makes the
sound *J* in Greek. Again, in order to make that sound Greek has
to resort to a combination of letters. In this case they are **T** and **Z**.
Together they make exactly the same kind of sound you'd expect
to find in Jackie, John and James.

Other Greek words which use the letters **TZ** or **τζ** in their lower-
case form are:

Τζατζίκι and Τζαζ

Exercise 3

See if you can have a go at this combination by completing the
half-written Greek versions of the English names below.

1	Jake Tod	ΤΖΕΙ_ΤΟ_Τ
2	Jasper Carrot	ΤΖΑ__ΕΡ ΚΑΡΡΟ_
3	James Bond	ΤΖΕΙΜΣ ΜΠΟ_Τ
4	Jill Ireland	__ΙΛ ΑΙΡΛΑ__
5	James Cooper	_____ ΚΟΥΠ__
6	Jackie Onassis	ΤΖΑ__ ΟΝΑΣΣΗ_
7	John Wayne	ΤΖΟΝ Γ__ΕΙΝ

Exercise 4

This is where it gets hard. On the following page is a handwritten recipe for a home-baked apple pie. Look at it carefully and see if you can identify and circle the ingredients from the list below:

Eggs	Αυγά
sugar	ζάχαρη
apples	μήλα
vanilla	βανίλια
milk	γάλα

Μηλόπιτα

υλικά :

4 Μήλα (τριμμένα)

2 φρυγανιές τριμμένες

1 κουταλιά γλυκού κανέλλα

1 φλυτζάνι τσαγιού ζάχαρη

1 βιτάμ

2 αυγά

1 ποτήρι νερού γάλα

1 βανίλλια

4 φλυτζάνια τσαγιού αλεύρι

Χτυπάμε τα αυγά με την ζάχαρη
μετά το βιτάμ λιωμένο, την
βανίλια, το γάλα και το αλεύρι.
Ανακατεύουμε όλα μαζί με τα
τριμμένα μήλα και γίνουμε
σε προθερμασμένο φούρνο 180°C.

Insight

Like most European languages Greek is under threat by the widespread use of the internet. The fact that many Greeks now use Latin characters to transliterate the sounds of Greek words when they communicate with each other has began to affect spelling and literacy amongst the Greek youth.

Exercise 5

Below is a list of some of the world's capital cities. They're all written in English but the Greek versions are all mixed up between lower- and upper-case letters, and some letters are missing. See if you can fill in the missing letters and then match the Greek words written in capitals with their lower-case letter counterpart.

1	WASHINGTON	ΜΕ_ΙΚΟ	Αθήνα
2	LONDON	ΑΘΗ_ _	Μα_ _ίτη
3	ATHENS	ΜΑΔΡΙΤΗ	Παρίσ_
4	MADRID	_ΑΡΙΣΙ	Ουάσινγκτον
5	PARIS	ΛΟΝ_Ι_Ο	_εξικό
6	MEXICO	ΟΥΑΣ_ _ΓΚΤΟ_	_ _νδίνο

Test yourself

You are fast becoming accustomed to reading Greek and understanding how to pronounce it. Because no effort should go unrewarded we are about to throw you in at the deep end. Below is a piece of Greek text. It contains some words you have not met before and many words you have. See if you can understand what it says. Don't worry! We have given you the answers at the back of the book, but give it your best shot before looking.

Θέλω ένα φλυτζάνι τσάι και ένα φλυτζάνι καφέ μαζί με την μηλόπιτα που παράγγειλα. Στο τσάι θέλω λίγο γάλα αλλά όχι ζάχαρη και στο καφέ θέλω ζάχαρη αλλά όχι γάλα.

Remember that there is no single letter which gives you the 'j' sound in Greek. Also remember that when Greeks pronounce 'j' they do so at the front of the mouth rather than the slightly more guttural 'j' we use. This gives it a more emphatic, flat sound which accounts for the 'Greek' accent when speaking English or pronouncing foreign words.

9

·····································

Ταξιδάκια
Little trips

In this unit you will learn
- *The letter combinations ΓΓ and ΓΚ*

Exercise 1

Mike and Lisa are really enjoying each other's company. They're enjoying each other's company so much in fact that at the end of a hectic few days' touring they discovered they weren't sure where they went on which days.

ΙΕΡΑ ΜΟΝΗ
ΤΑΞΙΑΡΧΟΥ ΜΙΧΑΗΛ ΤΟΥ ΠΑΝΟΡΜΙΤΟΥ
85600 ΣΥΜΗ – ΔΩΔΕΚΑΝΗΣΟΣ

ΜΟΥΣΕΙΑ : (ΕΚΚΛΗΣΙΑΣΤΙΚΟ – ΛΑΟΓΡΑΦΙΚΟ)
MUSEUMS : (ECCLESIASTICAL – FOLKLORE)

ΕΙΣΙΤΗΡΙΟ
TICKET

ΕΥΡΩ 0,20   № 01901
EURO €0.20

Their itinerary was chosen from the list of excursions on offer printed in Greek below. See if you can help them by finding out which package they took. The only clues Mike and Lisa have in their hazy memories are the three sets of tickets they found in their pockets!

Δελφοί. Η Θόλος στο ιερό της Αθηνάς Προναίας. Αρχές 4ου αι. π.Χ.
Delphi. Tholos in the sanctuary of Athena Pronaia. Beginning of 4th c. BC.

ΑΡΧΑΙΟΛΟΓΙΚΟΣ ΧΩΡΟΣ ΔΕΛΦΩΝ
ARCHAEOLOGICAL SITE OF DELPHI

ΑΧΔ 0359827

ΕΙΣΙΤΗΡΙΟ
ΕΙΣΟΔΟΥ

ΔΡΧ. 1.200
DRS.

ΕΝΤRΑΝCE
T I C K E T

Παρακαλείστε να κρατήσετε το απόκομμα του εισιτηρίου σας μέχρι την έξοδο σας από το χώρο.
You are requested to preserve your ticket until you leave the Museum/Site

Ημερομ.
/ / MAI. 1999

№ 4105

ΠΝΕΥΜΑΤΙΚΟ ΙΔΡΥΜΑ ΣΑΜΟΥ

"ΝΙΚΟΛΑΟΣ ΔΗΜΗΤΡΙΟΥ"
ΛΑΟΓΡΑΦΙΚΟ ΜΟΥΣΕΙΟ

ΕΙΣΙΤΗΡΙΟ ΕΙΣΟΔΟΥ
Δρχ. 500
ENTRANCE TICKET

Πυθαγόρειο 83103 Σάμος
Τηλ. (0273) 62286   Fax 62287

ΔΕΥΤΕΡΑ	ΤΡΙΤΗ	ΤΕΤΑΡΤΗ
Ξενοδοχείο	Ξενοδοχείο	Ξενοδοχείο
Δωδεκάνησα	Δελφοί	Δελφοί
Μουσείο – Αθήνα	Σάμος	Σάμος
Ταβέρνα	Εστιατόρειο	Δωδεκάνησα
Ξενοδοχείο	Ξενοδοχείο	Ξενοδοχείο

Insight

In keeping with the rest of Europe, some Greeks have become very affluent and travel abroad much more than they used to.

Exercise 2

This is the part where we give you the opportunity to show us how good you are. We have a word-search exercise below. Find the words from the list below and circle them so they join up. When you have done that you should have the outline of four Greek capital letters. When you rearrange them discover what word they spell.

The words which you need to find are:

ψωμί   λαός   γάλα   λάδι   ωμέγα   σήμα   γιατί   θέλω
ιδέα   αλάτι   ψάρι   κάνω

Γ	Α	Λ	Α	Β	Γ	Α	Ρ	Ψ	Υ	Λ	Β
Ι	Ρ	Α	Λ	Α	Λ	Μ	Α	Γ	Ω	Ρ	Α
Α	Μ	Π	Α	Ζ	Υ	Ρ	Γ	Ο	Δ	Μ	Τ
Τ	Γ	Ι	Τ	Ο	Ι	Υ	Ρ	Γ	Ι	Α	Ι
Ι	Ψ	Ρ	Ι	Τ	Θ	Ρ	Ι	Τ	Α	Ξ	Κ
Π	Λ	Ο	Υ	Σ	Α	Ε	Ε	Φ	Τ	Α	Δ
Α	Ι	Μ	Π	Α	Ρ	Γ	Λ	Δ	Ν	Υ	Σ
Π	Ο	Τ	Ο	Ψ	Μ	Ν	Ι	Ω	Ω	Μ	Α
Λ	Α	Ο	Σ	Μ	Π	Ι	Ν	Μ	Ρ	Ε	Φ
Α	Ρ	Λ	Η	Μ	Ο	Ν	Ι	Ε	Ε	Ν	Α
Δ	Ε	Ν	Μ	Π	Υ	Ρ	Α	Γ	Κ	Ι	Ν
Ι	Δ	Ε	Α	Κ	Α	Κ	Ο	Α	Α	Μ	Δ

The missing link

Up to now we have covered all the letters of the Greek alphabet and have managed to keep our promise to make them easy and fun. We did warn you that there was one Greek letter (just one) which can cause a few problems.

The gallows shadow of the letter Γ (gamma) takes a little getting used to. We left until now the last combination of letters that gamma forms to make the sound *g*.

If the sound appears in the middle of a word, then *G* is formed by **ΓΓ**.

Example: ENGLAND = ΑΓΓΛΙΑ

If the sound appears at the beginning of a word, then *G* is formed by **ΓΚ**.

Example: GREY = ΓΚΡΙΖΟ

Other words in Greek where the *g* sound appears are:

ΑΓΓΟΥΡΙ	*cucumber*	**ΑΓΓΙΖΩ**	*I touch*
ΑΓΓΕΛΟΣ	*angel*	**ΑΓΓΛΟΣ**	*Englishman*

Exercise 3

Now it's your turn. Write the words in the vocabulary box above in lower-case letters.

☑ Greece, the home of democracy, has never really had a 'free' press. Traditionally newspapers were strongly affiliated to different political parties which financed them and, therefore, controlled their editorial content. Their readership came from the parties' membership and the

Κυριακάτικη

ΕΛΕΥΘΕΡΟΤΥΠΙΑ

Β' ΕΚΔΟΣΗ

31 ΙΑΝΟΥΑΡΙΟΥ 1999 Περίοδος Β' • Αρ. φύλλου 1.096 • Δρχ. 250

Ο «ΚΑΙΡΟΣ» 2. ΠΟΛΙΤΙΚΗ 4. ΠΑΡΑΣΚΗΝΙΑ 18. ΚΟΣΜΟΣ 20. ΑRT 41. ΡΕΠΟΡΤΑΖ 72. ΣΠΟΡ 104.

ΕΝΑΣ ΣΤΟΥΣ ΔΕΚΑ πολίτες επενδύουν στο Χρηματιστήριο

ΕΛΛΗΝΙΚΗ ΤΡΕΛΑ ΜΕ ΤΟ ΧΡΗΜΑ

■ Νέο φαινόμενο το «κόμμα των κωδικών», αναδιατάσσει την τακτική της κυβέρνησης

Σ ε μία ακόμα πρωτόγνωρη πραγματικότητα οδηγεί η νεοελληνική κοινωνία οι εξελίξεις στην οικονομία. Ένας στους 5 ενεργούς πολίτες προσδοκά από κάποια από το Χρηματιστήριο, διαμορφώνοντας και μία νέου τύπου πολιτική οντότητα. Αυτήν ακριβώς μελέτουν τώρα τα κόμματα. ΣΕΛ. 4

ΕΞΤΡΑ ΕΚΔΟΣΗ ΤΗΣ «Κ.Ε.»

Τα μυστικά της ασφάλισης

Ειδικά τεσελίδο ένθετο για όλες τις ιδιωτικές ασφαλίσεις

Πίνακες και παραδείγματα για διαρκεώση, αλλα και επενδύσεις

ΜΙΑ ΝΕΑ ΣΠΑΝΙΑ ΠΡΟΣΦΟΡΑ

Η ΑΛΛΗ ΟΨΗ ΤΗΣ ΠΑΙΔΕΙΑΣ

Πρώτοι στο μάθημα πρώτοι στον αγώνα

Το πολύ σχολείο δεν: Δίκαια υπό κατάληψη έχουν «πρακτο» σε ΛΕΙ

Ο παπα-μπλόκος των καταλήψεων

Αγαπάει τους μαθητές, αλλα κάνει τον ...δρακουλόφο όταν κλείνουν οι θρανοί

newspaper was little more than a channel for propaganda. It is only in recent years that there has been a break from this practice, and newspapers are beginning to give a more balanced view of what is happening in Greek public life.

Insight

Politics continue to play a significant part in Greek life and the Greek lifestyle.

Exercise 4

While in Greece, Mike and Lisa spent some time in Athens. Ever ambitious, Mike picked up some newspapers. Look at the front page of Sunday's ΕΛΕΥΘΕΡΟΤΥΠΙΑ in Unit 9.

See if you can find the Greek words from the list below, then circle them. We decided to be tough and have given you the list in English. Good luck!

politics   sport   pullover   ten

Exercise 5

Mike and Lisa availed themselves of an offer to see as many islands as they could in one day. There is a map of their journey in the following pages. They both kept a diary of that day but the good wine and the warm sun did not help their Greek spelling. Perhaps you can help by deciphering exactly where they went that day. Follow their route and then fill in the missing letters from the words below to find out the names of the islands Mike and Lisa visited. Once you have filled in the missing letters re-write the islands in lower-case letters.

1 ΚΡ_Τ_
2 ΚΑ_ΟΣ

3 ΚΑΡΠ_ _ _ Σ
4 Χ_ΛΚ_
5 ΡΟ_ΟΣ
6 Σ_Μ_
7 ΤΗ_ _ Σ
8 ΝΙ _ _ ΡΟΣ

Insight

Traditional Greek cooking is slowly being lost as convenience foods and fast food shops proliferate in mainlaind Greece. However, we hope that your success in getting this far will encourage you to learn more of this fascinating language, so that you can perhaps venture off the well worn tourist tracks to discover that little, family-run ταβέρνα, just waiting for you, where the cooking is just like γιάγια (Granny) used to make ...

Exercise 6

On their day out to the islands, Mike and Lisa felt hungry. Unfortunately, they forgot to take enough money with them. Between them they had €9,oo. From the menu below, work out what they could have ordered from the restaurant in order to have as balanced a meal as possible.

Μπύρες

Gösser ποτήρι 330 ml	€2,50
Gösser ποτήρι 500 ml	€3,00
Heineken	€2,50
Mythos	€2,50
Kaiser	€2,50
Stella Artois	€2,50
Amstel	€2,50

Αναψυκτικά

Coca Cola	€2,00
Sprite	€2,00
Πορτοκαλάδα	€2,00
Λεμονάδα	€2,00
Σόδα	€2,00
Μεταλλικό νερό	€1,50
Εμφιαλωμένο νερό 1½ λίτρο	€1,75
Εμφιαλωμένο νερό ½ λίτρο	€0,50

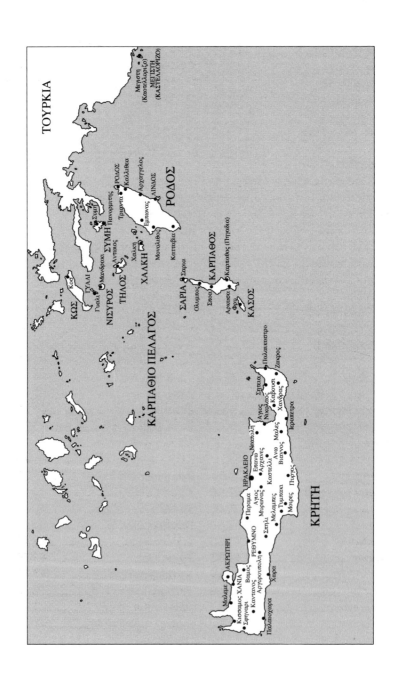

ΤΟΥΡΚΙΑ

Μεγίστη
(Καστελλόριζο)
ΜΕΓΙΣΤΗ
(ΚΑΣΤΕΛΛΟΡΙΖΟ)

Πανορμίτης
Τριανδα ΡΟΔΟΣ Κολυμπια
Σύμη Αρχάγγελος
Μονόβρα ΛΙΝΔΟΣ
Αντικας ΡΟΔΟΣ
Εμπωνάς
ΤΗΛΟΣ Χαλκη
Αληταριος Μονόλιθος
ΧΑΛΚΗ Καταβια

Γυαλι
Ποελι ΚΩΣ Κάσο
ΓΥΑΛΙ

ΝΙΣΥΡΟΣ ΣΑΡΙΑ Σαρια
ΚΑΡΠΑΘΟΣ
Ολυμπος Καρπαθος (Πηγάδια)
Σπόα
Αρκάσα ΚΑΣΟΣ
Φρυ

ΚΑΡΠΑΘΙΟ ΠΕΛΑΓΟΣ

Πελακαστρο
Σητεια Ζακρος
Αγιος
Νικόλαος Καψαλος
Χανδρος
Μοχλος Χανδρας
Ανω Ιεραπετρα
Βιαννος

ΗΡΑΚΛΕΙΟ Νεαπολι
Επανω Αρχανες
Περαμα Αγιος Καστελλι
Μυρωνας
Σπήλι Μελιδόνι Μοιρες Πυργος
Βαμος Τυμπακι
ΧΑΝΙΑ Κοντομαρι Χαρα
Μολεμε ΑΚΡΩΤΗΡΙ
Κισσαμος Σερφυγαρι ΡΕΘΥΜΝΟ
Καντανρη Αργυρουπολη
Παλαιοχωρα

ΚΡΗΤΗ

Ούζο (καραφάκι) €2,00

....

....

....

Κρασί χύμα (το κιλό) €3,50

....

....

....

ΚΡΑΣΙΑ
Λευκά
Πελοποννησιακός €6,00
Αγιορείτικο €8,80
Κτήμα Χατζημιχάλη €10,50
Ασπρολίθι €10,50
Μαντινεία €9,50
Δροσαλίς €8,00
Δώρα Διονύσιου €11,00
Ροδίτης Αλεπού €7,50
Εράσμιος €8,50

....

....

Ροζέi
Μοναστηριακό €9,70
Αλλοτινό €10,50
Εσπερίτης €7,50

....

Κόκκινα
Δάφνις €11,00
Κατώγι Αβέρωφ €15,25
Αμπελοχώρα €9,50
Σατυρικό €9,00

....

Ροζέ
Ουίσκυ €5,00
Ουίσκυ σπέσιαλ €6,00
Βατκα €5,00
Τζιν €5,00
Μαρτίνι €5,00
Campari €5,00
Λικέρ €7,00

....

Ορεχτικά
Πιπεριές γεμιστές €2,70
Σαγανάκι €2,00
Μπουρεκάκια €2,30
Κολοκυθοκεφτέδες €2,00
Κοτοκροκέτες €2,80
Κολοκυθόπιτα €3,00
Κεφτεδάκια €2,50
Τυροπιτάκια €2,00
Πατάτες μερίδα €1,00
Φέτα €1,50
Φέτα ψητή €1,50
Χορτόπιτα €2,70
Μπουρεκάκια του Σεφ €2,70
   (τυροκροκέτες)
Ριζότο πικάντικο €2,70
Μανιτάρια α λα κρεμ €3,50

....

Σαλάτες
Σεφ €3,70
Χωριάτικη €3,50
Τονοσαλάτα €2,10
Πατατοσαλάτα €2,70
Σαλάτα "Επιούσιος" €3,00

....

Κρέπες
Κοτόπουλο.................. €3,70
Κιμάς, πιπεριά, μανιτάρια.. €3,70
Ποικιλία ατομική.................. €5,00
....
....

Κύριο Πιάτο
Κοτόπουλο "Επιούσιος"........ €5,50
Κοτόπουλο σουβλάκι............ €4,10
Κοτόπουλο φιλέτο................. €4,00
Κοτόπουλο α λα κρεμ............ €4,70
Μπιφτέκι σχάρας.................. €3,50
Μπιφτέκι α λα κρεμ.............. €4,70
Μπιφτέκι
(γεμιστό με τυρί και ζαμπόν) €4,40

Μπιφτέκι με ροκφόρ............. €4,40
Σνίτσελ κοτόπουλο................ €4,70
Σνίτσελ χοιρινό.................... €4,10
Μπιζόλα χοιρινή.................... €3,80
Σουβλάκι χοιρινό (μερίδα)   €4,10
Λουκάνικο γεμιστό................ €3,90
....

Ζυμαρικά
Καρμπονάρα..................... €4,80
Σεφ................................. €4,80
Φούρνου.......................... €4,50
Πένες 4 τυριά.................... €4,80
Μπολονέζ.......................... €4,20
Ναπολιτέν.........................€4,70
....

....

Test yourself

Now that you are getting good it will be interesting to see just how good you are. We have given you different sections of a menu here which have got mixed up so that the starters do not appear at the beginning as they should. Decide how they should be rearranged so that the menu sections appear in a logical sequence:

Κύριο Πιάτο,   Αναψυκτικά,   Ζυμαρικά,
Ορεχτικά,   Σαλάτες,   Κρασιά,

10

Σουβενίρ
Souvenirs

In this unit you will learn
- *About Greek homophones*
- *To describe the weather*

No matter how good something is, sooner or later it has to come to an end. This book is no exception. Mike and Lisa, just like you, are now able to recognize practically any combination of Greek letters and pronounce a Greek word, even if they're not too sure about the meaning.

As the days approach for their leaving Greece, they begin to look for souvenirs which will remind them of their wonderful holiday.

The Greek word for 'souvenir' is very easy to recognize: ΣΟΥΒΕΝΙΡ. Now that you know it in capital form, and before we go any further, it might be a good idea if you wrote it in lower-case letters and decided where the stress should go.

Insight
Selling souvenirs to tourists used to be a sizeable cottage industry. It has now become a slowly fading tradition as other service sector activities are springing up to replace it.

Exercise 1

One of the things Mike and Lisa learnt soon after they started to read Greek was that the language has many words which sound nearly identical but have different meanings. The English prefix 'homo' for example comes from the Greek word ΟΜΟΙΟ meaning 'the same/identical'. When added to the word ΦΩΝΗ and suitably altered to sound smoother it becomes ΟΜΟΦΩΝΗ. Homophones, in English, are words with virtually the same pronunciation and different meanings. When it comes to it, though, the Greeks are masters at it. Consider, for example, the following list of pairs of ten virtually identical-sounding words written in capitals and lower-case letters. To find their meaning, all you have to do is identify their numbered counterpart from the box below.

1 χαρτί		**6** ΚΡΗΤΗ	
2 ΧΑΡΤΗΣ		**7** κρίνω	
3 βάζο		**8** ΚΡΙΝΟΣ	
4 ΒΑΖΩ		**9** φύλο	
5 κριτής		**10** ΦΙΛΟΣ	

> 10 *friend* (M) 1 *paper* 9 *sex* (M or F) 8 *lily* 3 *vase*
> 6 *Crete* (the island) 7 *I judge* 4 *I put* 2 *map* 5 *judge*

Now reverse the way the ten words are written so that the ones in capital letters are now written in lower-case letters and vice versa.

☑ If you're having trouble with homophones, spare a little sympathy for the Greeks themselves. The worst case of a homophone is given to us by the instance of the word for 'hand' which in very formal Greek (occasionally referred to by the misnomer of 'High Greek') is χείρα. Unfortunately for the Greeks the word for 'sow' (i.e. a female pig) sounds exactly the same although it is spelt χοίρα (you begin to realize now why there is a need for so many forms of the letter *i*). You will realize just how bad things get when we tell you that the word for 'widow' is also ... you guessed it ... χήρα!

Now in the days when students from all over Greece had to leave the family home and go away to Athens to study at the university there, it would not be unusual to run out of funds very quickly and have to write a hasty, and somewhat pleading, letter home asking for an advance on the following month's allowance. As it was usual, in those days, for the father to handle all family finances it was to him that the letter was addressed and it always finished with the conventional, but somewhat unfortunately chosen, 'I kiss your hand', just before the signature.

Given that there were three possible ways to spell a word which sounds exactly the same, the unfortunate students had a one-in-three chance of getting it right and being bailed out of debt!

Exercise 2

Mike and Lisa have decided to split the souvenirs they buy into three types: ones you can drink, ones you can eat and those bought as mementoes. The problem is that they're now having difficulty remembering any of the Greek words for the things they want to buy. See if you can help them out by writing a list from your own memory. Once you have exhausted the words you know you can look at the box at the bottom of this exercise for inspiration. A couple of words will be totally new to you, though by now you're more than adept at figuring them out!

Souvenirs

1   Things you drink   **2**   Things you eat   **3**   Mementoes

A little help: ούζο, Ελληνικός καφές, άγαλμα, χάρτης, ρετσίνα, φωτογραφία, μπλουζάκι, σημαία, εφημερίδα, γλυκά, βιβλία, εισιτήρια, ψώνια, δραχμές, σοκολάτα, Ελληνικό λάδι, πορτοκαλάδα, μπύρα, κασέτα, τσάντα

Greek weather

The weather in Greece is not always as good as tourists seem to think, although sunshine can more or less be guaranteed. The word for 'hot' in Greek is θερμός and from that are derived the words for 'temperature' – θερμοκρασία – and 'thermometer' – θερμόμετρο.

Insight

Global warming is making itself felt in Greece also. During the writing of this book summer temperatures were over 37 degrees Celsius each day.

Exercise 3

On their last day in Greece, Mike and Lisa look at a weather report in a local εφημερίδα to decide what to do. Look at the chart below. From the key find the Greek words for the following:

1 Sunny
2 Occasional cloud
3 Heavy cloud
4 Rain
5 Thunderstorm
6 Snow
7 Fog

From the same weather report write in capitals the names of the large cities, outside Greece, which have a temperature higher than London.

Now write in capitals the names of the Greek towns which have the same temperature as Rome.

Now write the name of the town whose temperature is nearest that of London.

ΘΕΡΜΟΚΡΑΣΙΕΣ	
Καβάλα	28
Κέρκυρα	30
Ηράκλειο	30
Λαμία	34
Πάτρα	34

Εξωτερικού	
Λονδίνο	22
Παρίσι	25
Ρώμη	34
Ζυρίχη	26
Μόσχα	24

ΑΙΘΡΙΟΣ

ΑΣΤΑΤΟΣ

ΣΥΝΝΕΦΙΑ

ΒΡΟΧΗ

ΚΑΤΑΙΓΙΔΑ

ΧΙΟΝΙ

ΟΜΙΧΛΗ

ΘΑΛΑΣΣΑ

ΗΡΕΜΗ

ΤΑΡΑΓΜΕΝΗ

ΠΟΛΥ ΤΑΡΑΓΜΕΝΗ

ΚΥΜΑΤΩΔΗΣ

ΤΡΙΚΥΜΙΩΔΗΣ

ΑΝΕΜΟΙ

ΑΣΘΕΝΕΙΣ

ΜΕΤΡΙΟΙ

ΙΣΧΥΡΟΙ

ΠΟΛΥ ΙΣΧΥΡΟΙ

ΘΥΕΛΛΩΔΕΙΣ

Acronyms

As the name suggests, acronyms (like acropolis) are quite literally the 'edges of names' or words which, as it happens, are usually defined by their first letters. The Greek word for 'name' is ONOMA and an 'acronym' in Greek is ΑΚΡΩΝΥΜΟ. By far the most famous (and maybe, initially, the most mystifying) acronym of all time has to be ΙΧΘΥΣ. It is usually found written inside the universal outline of a fish and it has stood for the sign for a Christian for at least the last two thousand years.

Indeed, ιχθύς does mean 'fish'. The reason it also stands for a follower of Christianity is that the letters, which coincidentally form the word fish, are themselves an acronym: ΙΗΣΟΥΣ ΧΡΙΣΤΟΣ, ΘΕΟΥ ΥΙΟΣ, ΣΩΤΗΡ (Jesus Christ, Son of God, Saviour). The acronym becomes even more evident if you rewrite the above sentence in lower-case letters but keep the first letter of each word as a capital.

Exercise 4

In their search for souvenirs Mike and Lisa wandered into a shop which sells popular Greek music. They each have €50 and this is the sum total of their money. See if you can help them choose a couple of CDs each from the selection on the opposite page so that they have some money left over for the flight.

More souvenirs

Mike and Lisa also bought a packet of the local Turkish Delight (a remnant of the times when Greece was a principality of the Ottoman empire), although they call it Greek Delight.

Because Mike is curious he has made a list of all the ingredients used in the Greek Delight. Circle the ones you recognize from the list Mike has made and then rewrite them using only capitals.

Ζάχαρη – Νερό – Βανίλια – Ζελατίνα

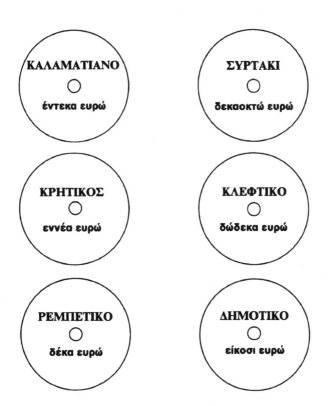

ΚΑΛΑΜΑΤΙΑΝΟ
έντεκα ευρώ

ΣΥΡΤΑΚΙ
δεκαοκτώ ευρώ

ΚΡΗΤΙΚΟΣ
εννέα ευρώ

ΚΛΕΦΤΙΚΟ
δώδεκα ευρώ

ΡΕΜΠΕΤΙΚΟ
δέκα ευρώ

ΔΗΜΟΤΙΚΟ
είκοσι ευρώ

Insight

Anagrams, or perhaps we should say αναγραμματισμός, owe much of their appeal to the third-century Greek poet Lycophon who popularized them in his work as part of an exercise in intellectual elegance. Ancient Greeks took particular delight in the flexibility of their language and its ability to challenge and entertain and began the tradition which was to be emulated so widely by so many other cultures throughout the centuries. It was during the reign of Queen Victoria that the Greek trait for creating anagrams and clever wordplay was rediscovered and elevated to new heights, albeit, this time, in English.

Exercise 5

The Greek word for postcard is καρτ-ποστάλ. Prior to leaving Greece Lisa buys a postcard to leave at her apartment with a thank you on the back. Because she has tried very hard throughout the holiday, Lisa has become quite proficient at writing out lower-case Greek. On the back of the postcard she has written:

Should there be something here?

To διαμέρισμα
ηταν πολύ ωραίο.
Ευχαριστώ για
όλα.
- Λίζα

The flat was very nice.

Thank you for everything.

Lisa

See if you can copy what she has written using only capital letters.

Exercise 6

Mike and Lisa's holiday has gone far better than they'd planned. As a matter of fact it's gone so well that they decide to come back next year, together! Mike has gone ahead and bought a map to help them decide where to go. He chose the wrong map, however, as it only lists a small group of islands, near Turkey! Look at the map on the following pages and then write, in capital letters, the names of the islands in the order the ferry visits them (Lesbos – Chios – Psara) and then the main city on each island.

Exercise 7

Mike and Lisa are getting ready to leave for Athens airport where a flight is waiting to get them home. They find that, in order to get there, they have to reverse their outward journey. They first need a boat, then a taxi and finally, an aeroplane. Their transportation is written below in capitals. Unfortunately, however, some of the letters have been scrambled (did we mention that anagram is a Greek word – ανάγραμμα?). To help you unscramble them, we have provided a key, but the key, which is in lower-case letters, has been partially destroyed, so that some letters are missing. See if you can match the missing letters with the scrambled words so that you can write out the word in full:

KABAPI   _ αρά _ _
ΑΕΠΑΡΛΟΝΟ   αερ _ _ λά _ _
ΙΞΤΑ   _ _ ξ _

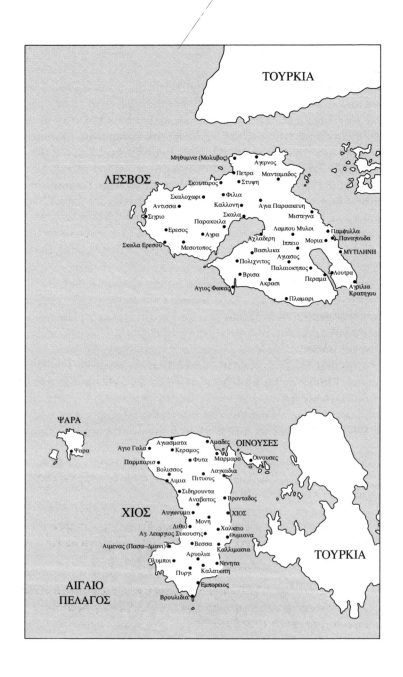

ΤΟΥΡΚΙΑ

ΛΕΣΒΟΣ

Μηθυμνα (Μολυβος)
Αγερνος
Πετρα
Μανταμαδος
Σκουταρος
Στυψη
Φιλια
Σκαλοχωρι
Αντισσα
Καλλονη
Αγια Παρασκευη
Σιγρι
Σκαλα
Μιστεγνα
Παρακοιλα
Ερεσος
Λαμπου Μυλοι
Παμφυλλα
Αγρα
Αχλαδερη
Ιππειο
Μορια
Παναγιουδα
Σκαλα Ερεσου
Μεσοτοπος
Βασιλικα
ΜΥΤΙΛΗΝΗ
Πολιχνιτος
Αγιασος
Παλαιοκηπος
Λουτρα
Βρισα
Αγρilια
Ακρασι
Περαμα
Κρατηγου
Αγιος Φωκας
Πλωμαρι

ΨΑΡΑ

Ψαρα

Αγιασματα
Αμαδες
ΟΙΝΟΥΣΕΣ
Αγιο Γαλα
Κεραμος
Μαρμαρο
Οινουσες
Παρμπαριο
Φυτα
Βολισσος
Λαγκαδια
Λιμια
Πιτυους
Σιδηρουντα
Αναβατος
Βροντaδος
ΧΙΟΣ
Αυγωνυμα
ΧΙΟΣ
Μονη
Λιθιο
Χαλκειο
Αγ. Λεωργιος Συκουσης
Θυμιανα
Αιμενας (Πασα–Δμανι)
Βεσσα
Καλλιμασια
ΤΟΥΡΚΙΑ
Αρμολια
Ολυμποι
Νενητα
Πυργι
Καλαυωτη
Εμπορειος
ΑΙΓΑΙΟ
ΠΕΛΑΓΟΣ
Βρουλιδια

Test yourself

So far you've got through everything with flying colours. So it really is time to celebrate, which is why we are going to break out the κρασί (accompanied by some suitable snacks or μεζές – of course). In the text below we have given you the recipe for a starter which goes with pretty much any Greek wine. It is all in Greek and has a sprinkling of words you've never encountered before. See how you do (you may find yourself being able to read the words without completely understanding them):

1 κιλό κολοκύθια
500 γραμμ. πατάτες
500 γραμμ. φέτα σε τρίμμα
5 αβγά
4 κ.σ. αλεύρι
40 γραμμ. γραβιέρα ή άλλο σκληρό τυρί
½ ματσάκι δυόσμο, μόνο τα φύλλα ψιλοκομμένα
Αλάτι, πιπέρι

1 Προθερμάνετε το φούρνο στους 200° C.

2 Καθαρίστε τα κολοκύθια και τις πατάτες και τρίψτε τα στο χοντρό του τρίφτη. Στίψτε τα καλά σε ένα σουρωτήρι για να χάσουν όσο δυνατόν περισσότερα υγρά.

3 Σε ένα μπολ ανακατέψτε όλα τα υλικά. Το δυόσμο μπορείτε να τον αντικαταστήσετε ή να τον μειώσετε ανάλογα με τις προτιμήσεις σας.

4 Βουτυρώστε ένα μεγάλο πυρίμαχο ταψί, γεμίστε το με το μίγμα και τρίψτε από πάνω τη γραβιέρα που θα δημιουργήσει μια ωραία χρυσαφένια κρούστα.

5 Ψήστε μέχρι να ροδίσει η «ομελέτα» από πάνω, περίπου 45–60 λεπτά.

6 Αφήστε την ομελέτα να κρυώσει, κόψτε την κομμάτια και βάλτε τη στο ψυγείο μέχρι να τη χρειαστείτε.

But so that we don't give you heartburn, you will find the words which may have proved indigestible in the Key at the end of the book.

Now look at the Glossary for the second half of the book, starting at p. 117. We hope you are impressed by the amount you have learnt.

Γλωσσάριο
Glossary

Glossary is a Greek word, and it comes from the word ΓΛΩΣΣΑ (glossa), meaning 'tongue'. In Greek it also means 'language'. To the ancient Greek mind, language and tongue were so closely connected that they were indistinguishable, and this is something which is reflected in modern Greek today, as there is no other word for language apart from the word ΓΛΩΣΣΑ.

In the glossary that follows we give you the meaning of each word as a handy reference guide and also, where appropriate, its context as well as the capital letter it introduced. Our hope is that each word widens your window into the Greek culture, just as it enriches your knowledge of the Greek language.

Unit 1

ΤΑΞΙ – Ξ   *taxi*. Greek taxis work in taxi ranks but they also cruise the cities and towns as they can stop and pick up passengers anywhere, provided the 'taxi' sign on top of the cab is lit.

MINI – M   *mini*. Literally, the British cult car, but also a short skirt. The mini skirt became popular in Greece in the 60s and 70s along with the car. The latter was particularly suitable for driving through the narrow streets of Greek cities and towns and caused few problems in parking.

MONO – N   *alone* or *only*

NOTA – T   *a musical note*

ΜΑΞΙ – Ι   *a long skirt*. The opposite of a mini skirt.

ΠΑΝΩ – Ω *up*. In fact, ΠΑΝΩ is a popular contraction of the word ΕΠΑΝΩ. Many modern Greek words have dropped letters which are not pronounced any more because of popular usage.

ΚΑΤΩ – Ω *down*

ΚΑΖΑΝΙ – Ζ *cauldron*. Originally black cauldrons were used in Greek villages to do all the boiling in. This meant that they were used both for cooking food and doing the family laundry (which tended to be mainly grey and black colours). This is a practice that is encountered rarely these days and then only in the poorest villages.

ΚΟΜΜΑ – Κ *comma*

ΚΑΚΟ – Ο *bad*. This Greek word has become absorbed into English as a prefix to words such as 'cacophony' (itself a Greek compound word).

ΚΑΔΕΝΑ – Δ *neck* or *watch chain*, usually made of gold.

ΚΑΝΩ – Κ *I do/I make* and *I'm doing/I'm making*

ΕΔΩ – Ω *here*

ΔΥΟ – Υ *two*. Ancient Greeks were very interested in the concept of 'two' because they firmly believed that everything in the world existed in pairs. They saw good co-existing with bad, hot with cold and war with peace. This duality influenced western thought significantly and shaped our philosophies and even our political practices and theological beliefs for over 3,000 years.

ΔΕΞΙΑ – Δ *right* (as in direction). Words such as 'dexterity', 'dextrous' and even 'ambidextrous' bear witness to the fact that society has traditionally approved of right-handedness.

ΔΕΜΑ – Δ *parcel* or *packet*

ΔΕΚΑ – Δ *ten*

ΔΕΝ – Δ *not*

ΠΟΤΟ – Π *drink*. Alcohol in Greece is sold practically everywhere. There are no licensing laws restricting its sale and you can buy beer at two in the morning from your local deli, provided it's still open.

ΠΙΝΩ – Π *I drink/I'm drinking*

ΠΑΩ – Π *I go/I'm going*

ΠΑΚΕΤΟ – Π *packet* or *parcel*

ΕΝΑ – Ε *one*

ΕΞΙ – Ξ *six*. A two-dimensional shape with six sides is a hexagon.

ΕΠΤΑ – Π *seven*. Depending on where you go, you may hear the number seven pronounced as ΕΦΤΑ or ΕΠΤΑ. The variation in pronunciation may have been regional to start with, although it most probably occurred during the 400 years when Greece was part of the Ottoman Empire. There is no cultural stigma attached to either pronunciation and both are equally well understood.

ΟΚΤΩ – Ω *eight*. Again this may be pronounced as either ΟΚΤΩ or ΟΧΤΩ.

ΕΝΝΕΑ – Ε *nine*. Sometimes pronounced ΕΝΝΙΑ.

ΔΕΚΑ – Δ *ten*. In English we find it in such 'borrowed' words as decalogue.

ΔΩΔΕΚΑ – Δ *twelve*. A dodecahedron, in geometry, is a three dimensional twelve-sided object.

ΔΕΚΑΕΞΙ – Δ *sixteen*

ΔΕΚΑΕΠΤΑ – Δ *seventeen*. Again this one may be pronounced ΔΕΚΑΕΠΤΑ or ΔΕΚΑΕΦΤΑ.

ΔΕΚΑΟΚΤΩ – Ω *eighteen*. Pronounced either ΔΕΚΑΟΚΤΩ or ΔΕΚΑΟΧΤΩ.

ΤΟΞΟ – Ξ bow, as used in archery. 'Toxic' derives from the classical Greek word for arrow poison.

ΙΔΕΑ – Α *idea*. The ancient Greeks believed that ideas had an existence outside the world of the mind. They believed that, once grasped, they revealed something about the world which existed in the metaphysical realm. This provided Greek thinkers of the time with the ability to visualize and carry out complex thought experiments using no aid other than that of rigorous logic. While this helped them make some truly astounding discoveries, like the concept of atoms for example, it also hampered the appearance of the experimental method for many centuries.

ATOMO – A *atom* and *individual*. It was Democritus the Abderite (also known as the Laughing Philosopher, for his pleasant, easy-going approach to life) who first came up with the theory of atoms making up the world. Carrying out a thought experiment, Democritus visualized cutting things down into smaller pieces until he arrived at the concept of a spherical body so tiny that it could no longer be cut. The ancient Greek word for cut was TOMH and the prefix A- in front meant 'not'. Therefore ATOMO was something which literally could not be cut any further, or at least not without destroying its distinct identity, pretty much like individuals!

Unit 3

ENA – N   the number *one*

ΚΑΦΕ – Φ   *coffee* and the colour *brown*.

ΣΗΜΑ – H   *sign* and *badge*. It also means *signal*.

ΣΟΚ – Σ   *shock*. This is an imported word into Greek.

ΣΟΦΙΑ – Φ   *wisdom*. In ancient Greece there was an Olympian goddess called Wisdom and she was the one responsible for those who were wise.

ΛΑΟΣ – Λ   *people massed together*, and *race* as in a race of people.

ΛΑΔΙ – Λ   *oil*

ΕΛΕΟΣ – Λ   *mercy*. This is a word connected to the Greek word for oil, ΛΑΔΙ, because an olive wreath was given as a token of peace between the Greek city-states (at the end of an armed conflict).

ΠΟΛΥ – Λ   *very, a lot*

ΕΛΛΗΝΙΚΟΣ – Λ   *Greek*. It is also the name by which Greek coffee, a potent brew, is known. It used to be known as Turkish coffee (ΤΟΥΡΚΙΚΟΣ) until the early 1970s when relations between Turkey and Greece deteriorated. It was decided then that it should be known as Greek coffee, though quite a few people still persist in ordering it as Turkish coffee at their local coffee shop.

ΓΛΥΚΟ – Γ   *sweet*

ΓΑΛΑ – Γ   *milk*

ΓΙΑΤΙ – Γ   *why, because*. It is not unusual in Greek to answer a question beginning with ΓΙΑΤΙ with a sentence also beginning with ΓΙΑΤΙ.

ΓΙΑ – Γ   *for*

ΚΑΦΕΔΕΣ – Φ   *coffees*

ΝΕΡΟ – Ρ   *water*. In Greece, coffee is traditonally always accompanied with a glass of water.

ΝΕΡΑ – Ρ   the plural of water (whether it is a glass of water or water in general).

ΠΑΡΑΚΑΛΩ – Ω   *please*. In Greek, 'please' comes from a word which originally meant 'I beg'. Therefore, translated literally, **ΠΑΡΑΚΑΛΩ** means 'I beg of you'.

ΑΓΟΡΑ – Ρ   *a market*

ΑΓΟΡΑΖΩ – Ρ   *I buy/I'm buying*

ΟΥΖΟ – ΟΥ   ouzo, the fiery Greek drink.

ΟΥΖΕΡΙ –   a specialist outlet, traditionally cheap, where sailors and villagers would congregate to drink ouzo and listen to live music played on a mandolin.

ΚΡΑΣΙ – Σ   *wine*

ΤΕΚΙΛΑ – Λ   *tequila*

ΟΥΙΣΚΙ – ΟΥ   *whisky*

ΜΑΡΤΙΝΙ – Ρ   *martini*

ΛΕΜΟΝΑΔΑ – Δ   *lemonade*

ΠΟΡΤΟΚΑΛΑΔΑ – Π   *orangeade*

ΜΕΖΕΣ – Ζ   *tit bit*. The concept of ΜΕΖΕΣ was born out of necessity. In earlier times when refrigeration was a problem, eating places which served wine and ouzo were faced with the dilemma of what to serve with it. A ΜΕΖΕΣ can be anything from fried cheese to chips or meatballs.

ΣΑΓΑΝΑΚΙ – Γ   traditional ouzeri food. It consists of fried hard cheese and fried squid or octopus served in a light vinaigrette dressing.

ΟΚΤΑΠΟΔΙ – Δ   *octopus*. It literally means 'eight-legged'.

ΚΕΦΤΕΔΑΚΙΑ – Φ   *small meatballs*

ΠΑΤΑΤΕΣ – Π   *potatoes* and also *chips*

ΛΕΩΦΟΡΕΙΟ – ΕΙ   *bus*

ΘΕΛΩ – Θ   *I want*

ΘΕΛΕΙΣ – Θ   *you want*

ΘΕΛΕΙ – Θ   *he/she/it wants*

ΘΕΛΟΥΜΕ – Θ   *we want*

ΘΕΛΕΤΕ – Θ   *you want*

ΘΕΛΟΥΝΕ – Θ   *they want*

ΚΑΙ – ΑΙ   *and*

ΜΕ – Μ   *with*

ΜΠΑΡ – ΜΠ   *bar*. This is another one of those imported words. As modern Greek uses a combination of letters in order to reproduce the sound *B*, it makes for some very funny looks from English speakers when it's encountered on signs.

ΜΠΟΥΚΑΛΙ – ΜΠ   *bottle*

ΜΠΥΡΑ – ΜΠ   *beer*

ΜΠΟΥΚΑΛΙΑ – ΜΠ   *bottles*

ΠΙΤΣΑ – ΤΣ   *pizza*

ΠΙΤΣΑΡΙΑ – ΤΣ   the place where you would expect to buy a pizza.

ΚΑΦΕΤΕΡΙΑ – Φ   *a coffee shop*. Greek coffee shops tend to be very popular places and quite a lot of them will also do food like pizza and barbecued chicken with chips.

ΜΠΥΡΑΡΙΑ – ΜΠ   where you would go to drink beer and have a meze.

ΤΑΒΕΡΝΑ – Β   traditionally Greek tavernas served mainly wine, usually a number of local varieties straight from the barrel, as well as the Greek retsina.

ΒΙΒΛΙΟ – Β   *book*

ΒΑΖΟ – Β   *vase*

ΒΟΥΤΥΡΟ – ΟΥ   *butter*

ΔΡΑΧΜΗ – Χ   the old Greek currency.

ΕΚΑΤΟ – Ο   *a hundred*

Unit 4

ΧΙΛΙΑ – Χ   *a thousand*. ΧΙΛΙΑ has loaned itself, in a slightly altered form, into words such as 'kilometre' (a thousand metres) and 'kilogram' (a thousand grams).

ΨΑΡΙ – Ψ   *fish*

ΨΩΜΙ – Ψ   *bread*. In many places, Greek bread is still made in a stone-floored oven.

ΨΩΝΙΖΩ – Ψ   *I buy/I am buying*

ΦΡΟΥΤΟΠΩΛΕΙΟ – ΕΙ   a place where you would go to buy fresh produce. In Greece, for many years, such shops provided the only outlet available to local farmers. In many places they still do.

ΦΡΟΥΤΑ – ΟΥ *fruit*

ΤΥΡΟΠΩΛΕΙΟ – ΕΙ   a shop specializing in the sale of cheese. Cheese was usually kept in wooden caskets, in brine, to preserve it and you used to be able to try it before you bought it. Progress in the form of air-tight, sealed packaging is doing away with the few cheese shops which are left.

ΤΥΡΙ – Υ *cheese*

ΓΑΛΑΚΤΟΠΩΛΕΙΟ – ΕΙ   a shop selling only dairy produce such as eggs, milk and yoghurt. It would normally be run by the local milkman who would also have a delivery round in the area. Until the early 1970s the round would consist of a milk delivery in the morning and another delivery for yoghurt and eggs in the early evening. The milk is goat's or sheep's milk, and the yoghurt would have been made during the day by the milkman, hence the second delivery. Similarly, hens' eggs would have been laid and collected that day.

ΨΑΡΟΠΩΛΕΙΟ – Ψ   *a fishmonger's*. They were normally run by fishermen who would use them to sell their catch of the day.

Unit 5

ΩΡΑ – Ω   *time*. This word has become the basis for borrowed English words such as horoscope (which depends upon an accurate knowledge of one's time of birth in order to cast) and horology (the art of clockmaking).

ΨΩΝΙΑ – Ω   *the shopping*, i.e. things you have bought.

ΜΑΓΑΖΙ – Γ   *shop*. This is applied in a generic manner to any shop in Greece.

ΖΑΧΑΡΗ – Χ   *sugar*

ΡΕΤΣΙΝΑ – ΤΣ   the famous Greek wine, which takes its name from the resin now used to flavour it. It's believed that originally it came about when either wood resin from wine barrels which had not been properly cured or the resin used to seal them got into the wine by accident.

ΤΡΟΠΟΙ – ΟΙ   *manners, method, way*

ΣΥΜΠΕΡΙΦΟΡΑ – ΜΠ   *behaviour*

ΤΡΟΠΟΙ ΣΥΜΠΕΡΙΦΟΡΑΣ –   *manners*, literally 'way of behaviour'

ΕΥΓΕΝΗΣ – ΕΥ   *noble, polite*

ΕΥΓΕΝΕΙΑ – ΕΙ   *politeness* also *nobility*.

ΕΥΓΕΝΙΚΟΣ – ΕΥ   *polite*

ΕΥΧΑΡΙΣΤΩ – ΕΥ   *thank you*

ΕΥΚΟΛΟ – ΕΥ   *easy*

ΔΕΥΤΕΡΑ – ΕΥ   *Monday*. In Greek it literally means 'the second day of the week'.

ΑΥΓΑ – ΑΥ   *eggs*

ΑΛΑΤΙ – Λ   *salt*

ΠΙΠΕΡΙ – Π   *pepper*

ΝΤΟΜΑΤΕΣ – ΝΤ   *tomatoes*

ΟΜΕΛΕΤΑ – Λ   *omelette*. This is one of those words, which though borrowed, is now considered 'Greek' and follows the grammar of the Greek language.

ΑΜΕΡΙΚΗ – Η   *America*

ΙΤΑΛΙΑ – Ι   *Italy*

ΕΛΛΑΔΑ – Λ   *Greece*

ΙΑΠΩΝΙΑ – Π   *Japan*

ΚΟΡΕΑ – Ρ   *Korea*

ΑΥΣΤΡΑΛΙΑ – ΑΥ   *Australia*

Μεγάλα – γ *plural, big, large*. The Greek word for 'big' has lent itself in English to such words as 'megalomaniac' and the now popularly accepted slang prefix 'mega'.

Μικρά – κ *plural, small, little*. As with 'big', the Greek word for 'small' has found many applications in English, where we have imported derivatives such as 'microcosm', 'microscopic', 'micron' and 'microscope'.

Ντεντέκτιβ – ντ *detective*, though the word in Greek is popularly applied to private investigators and sleuths more than to police detectives. Peculiarly perhaps, the 'detective novel', in Greek, is called the 'police novel' or more popularly, 'police story'.

Πιτσαρία – τσ *a pizza restaurant*. Italy started out as an ancient Greek colony but in the course of time has come to influence a lot of the cultural aspects of modern Grece. This is reflected in the popularity of pizza and spaghetti in the Greek menu.

Ουζερί – ου a place where you would go to drink ouzo and have a meze. Modern ουζερί, in Athens and the islands, these days also offer live entertainment and a more varied drinks menu, though food remains fairly rudimentary in its variety.

Μπυραρία – μπ a place where you would go to drink mainly beer. These places were tremendously popular during the 60s and 70s when beer was the drink of choice of the 'flower power generation' in Greece. They are now slowly disappearing.

Καφετερία – φ a Greek café

Οπωροπωλείο – ω *a fruit shop*. It's a compound word from Οπωρικά (green produce) and πουλάω (I sell). Greek fruit shops portray an element of Greek life which sadly is slowly disappearing. They display a lot of their produce in the wooden crates it comes in, outside the shop. When the shop is closed, the owners cover the produce with tarpaulin but still leave it outside, overnight and unattended! This is a practice which is slowly dying out as specialized fruit shops become fewer in number and some of the less savoury aspects of modern life catch up in Greece.

Χρυσοχοείο – ει   *jeweller's*. It literally means 'gold-maker'. The Greek for 'gold' is χρυσός. Greek jewellery has a tradition which goes back more than 3,000 years. Greek gold jewellery is slightly heavier and darker in colour than gold jewellery in other parts of the world because Greek jewellers work with either 18 or 22 karat gold, not with 9kt.

Ξενοδοχείο – ει   *hotel*. A compound word (Ξένος = 'foreigner' and δοχείο = container) literally meaning 'a container for foreigners'! It has loaned itself to words such as 'xenophobia' (a fear of strangers).

Αρτοπωλείο – ω   *bakery*. Traditionally, in Greece, every neighbourhood had its own bakery where bread was freshly stone-baked on a daily basis.

Ζαχαροπλαστείο – ει   *pâtisserie*. Greek sweets make use of a lot of cream which itself is sweetened.

Εστιατόριο – ει   *restaurant*

Κινηματογράφος – η   *cinema*. Literally translated, it means 'writing in motion'.

Ντισκοτέκ – ντ   *disco*. While this is obviously the Greek equivalent of an imported word from English, there is a school of thought which says that the Greeks originally exported it to England in its Greek original which is δισκοθήκη = 'discotheque'. This is a compound word meaning 'container for music records'.

Φαρμακείο – ει   *pharmacy/chemist's*. Originally it took its name from the word φαρμάκι meaning poison, as in ancient Greece, many of the cures effected were through the use of diluted concoctions of otherwise poisonous substances.

Ταχυδρομείο – ει   *post office*. Given the problems that the Greek postal service has had over the past ten years in delivering things on time, the literal translation of this word (i.e. 'fast road') may be slightly ironic!

Φαγητό – η *food*

Ψωμί – ψ *bread*

Χρυσός – ς *gold*. Chrysanthemum (gold flower), and chrysalis (golden) which originally referred to a gold coloured butterfly pupa, are English derivatives.

Γλυκά – γ *sweets* (plural)

Δωμάτιο – δ *room*

Φιλμ – μ *movie/film*. English film titles do not always translate well into Greek, so many films appear with titles which bear no resemblance to the original.

Καφέ – κ *coffee*

Ασπιρίνη – Π *aspirin*

Χορός – ρ *dance*. This is directly linked to the English words 'chorus' and 'choir'. In ancient Greek plays the chorus and choir both sang and danced in the background in order to fill the transitional gaps in the play, or to tell the historical background, against which the drama of the play was unfolding.

Γραμματόσημα – μ *stamps*. It literally means 'a sign for a letter'.

Απογευματινή – ν Initially, a daily newspaper appearing only in Athens (as most papers did at the time), it's now a national paper.

Ακρόπολη – λ another influential Athenian daily paper. Others like it are Μεσημβρινή (lit. Noon paper), Σημεριανή (Today's paper), Κήρυκας (translated as perhaps slightly ambitious 'Gospel') and Εθνική (National).

Πελοπόννησος – ν a regional newspaper. As the name suggests it is limited to the Peloponnese area.

Γλυκός – ν *sweet* (adjective), as in a sweet coffee, etc.

Σιδηρόδρομος – δ *railway*. The railway did not come until fairly late in Greece and it's not the fastest means of travel across the country, though it is certainly amongst the cheapest. The word itself is a compound word and it means 'iron road'.

Σίδηρος – ρ *iron*

Δρόμος – μ *road*. While this word is used to describe a road, it is not the word you will see on the names of Greek road signs.

Τραίνο – αι *train*

Λεωφορείο – ει *bus*. Greece has an excellent public transport network. Although bus stops themselves are not always well signposted, the buses run every 15 minutes and they are inexpensive.

Αυτοκίνητο – αυ *car*, literally 'automatic motion'. There is no indigenous car industry in Greece and all makes have to be imported. Because Greece has a high level of tax avoidance, the Greek Inland Revenue uses car ownership to gauge levels of income (and therefore tax liability). The formula used in this instance centres on the size of the engine of the car you buy. This is only one reason why smaller cars are so popular in Greece.

Φεριμπότ – μπ *ferry* (boat). A word imported into Greek.

Ελικόπτερο – λ *helicopter*

Φορτηγό – Φ *truck*

Πούλμαν – ου *coach*

Τελεφερίκ – λ *cable car*

Υποβρύχιο – β *submarine*

Τανξ – ξ *tank*

Αεροπλάνο – ρ *aeroplane*

Ταξί – ξ *taxi*

Τυροπωλείο – υ a place that sells only cheese or dairy products.

Γαλακτοπωλείο – ει a place which sells exclusively milk products.

Βιβλιοπωλείο – β *a bookshop*. Though the ancient Greeks were in love with literature, there was never a thriving book trade at the time. The main reason for this was one of cost. In the days of ancient Greece, most writing was done on wax tablets, where letters were literally scratched on dark-coloured wax, which then allowed a lighter-coloured wood background to show through. Tablets were bound together using metal rings, looped through holes in their edges. The first organized, systematic buying and selling of books developed in Alexandria in the 2nd century BC primarily because of the influence of its famous library, run by Ptolemy.

Γάλα – γ   *milk*. Funnily enough, the Greek word for 'milk' is responsible for the naming of the Galaxy (Milky Way), where the first observers thought the broad band of stars through its middle looked like a streak of spilled milk.

Πορτοκάλι – π   *orange*. The same word is used for both the fruit and the colour, though the stress in the latter is shifted to the very last letter.

Ντομάτες – ντ   *tomatoes*

Μήλα – μ   *apples*

Τυρί – τ   *cheese*. The main types of cheese you buy in Greece are the produce of either sheep or goat's milk. Until the early 1900s there were three types of cheese which were described according to their hardness as soft, medium, and hard. Hard cheese would be cured in the open air for quite a long time. It was salty and only good for use in σαγανάκι where it would be accompanied by ouzo, or grated and sprinkled on food.

Μπουκάλι – μπ   *bottle*. Bottled wine in a taverna is a fairly novel concept in Greece, though restaurants have used bottles a lot longer. Traditionally, tavernas serve their wine straight from the barrel.

Κρασί – κ   *wine*

Βιβλίο – Β   *book*. The word has lent itself to such usage as 'bibliography' (writing about books or a list of books) and the Bible.

Φέτα – φ   a soft, white Greek cheese, made out of goat's milk, with a distinctive flavour and texture. Different regions of Greece produce different types of feta cheese.

Ουίσκυ – ου   *whisky*

Καρπούζι – ζ   *water melon*. Water melons in Greece are abundant during the summer months, where in many places they are sold from the back of farm trucks, by the side of roads, or near beaches.

Γιαούρτι – γ   *yoghurt*. Greek yoghurt is a very rich, full-fat yoghurt and is the usual dessert to a Greek meal. It is served sprinkled lightly with cinnamon, or topped with honey. Greek yoghurt is made from the milk of goats or sheep, not cows. Greece doesn't have many cows as its mountainous terrain cannot sustain the grasslands necessary for dairy herds.

Σοκολάτα – Σ   *chocolate*

Βούτυρο – η   *butter*

Πακέτο – π   *packet*

Μπισκότα – μπ   *biscuits*

Λεμόνια – λ   *lemons*

Μπύρα – μπ   *beer*

Unit 7

Τρώμε – ω   *We eat/We are eating*. Because eating out is so cheap, Greece has a thriving night-life. People think nothing of going out for a meal at least twice a week. Although tourist restaurants open early, Greek restaurant hours are somewhat later than ours, as many Greeks would not consider having their evening meal before ten o'clock!

Έξω – ξ   *out*. The word 'exodus' is derived directly from this.

Μενού – ου   *menu*. A word clearly imported into Greek from English.

Γεμιστά – Γ   *stuffed tomatoes* (usually). These are beef tomatoes with the insides emptied and the skin stuffed with rice and (depending in which region you have them) mince.

Πατάτες – Π   *potatoes* and also, *chips*. Potatoes were introduced in Greece in the late 1800s by Ioannis Metaxas. They were initially called γεώμηλα (earth-apples) because of their appearance and the then hungry populace, suspicious of anything introduced by the government, refused to eat them. The story goes that the Greek governor ordered mountains of potatoes to be piled high in public squares under guard. The guards were given specific instructions to look the other way should anyone try to steal them. Some of them were indeed stolen and presumably cooked and eaten. Word of mouth soon spread and the rest is history.

Φούρνου – φ   *oven baked*. Quite a lot of food is cooked this way in Greece.

Τηγανητές – η   *fried* (usually refers to chips)

Παστίτσιο – τσ   a pasta and mincemeat dish, the origins of which lie more in the East than Greece.

Μακαρονάδα – δ   *cooked spaghetti*

Μπριζόλα – μπ   *steak*. The traditional Greek diet is low on meat and very rich in vegetable dishes. Historically this is due to what was seasonally available to a population with no access to refrigeration.

Χοιρινή – χ   *pork*

Μοσχαρίσια – ρ   *beef*

Κεφτέδες – Κ   *meatballs*. Greek mince is made directly from prime cuts of meat which are then minced, so there is no compromise in quality.

Σαλάτα – τ   *salad*

Χωριάτικη – Χ   This is what is usually known as Greek salad, though the more literal translation is 'village salad'. Traditional Greek salad is rich in olive oil (a handy source of unsaturated fat) and it also contains feta cheese, tomatoes, cucumbers and olives.

It is, in many respects, a meal in itself and the olive oil that's in it is usually soaked up by bread and then eaten.

Μαρούλι – μ   *lettuce*

Φαστ Φουντ – Φ   *fast food*. Quite a few English words have been adopted by the Greeks as the globalization of a 'fast' lifestyle makes itself felt.

Χάμπουρκερ – Χ   *hamburger*

Σάντουιτς – Σ   the concept of the sandwich is relatively new in Greek culture and still considered something of a novelty in certain remote parts.

Σαλάτα – σ   *salad*. Interestingly, because the Greek salad has a lot of ingredients which need to be tossed, the phrase 'You've made a salad of it' is identical in meaning to the English 'you've made a hash of it'.

Σως – ω   *sauce*. It usually refers to tomato sauce.

Κετσάπ – τσ   *ketchup*

Μουστάρδα – δ   *mustard*. Greek mustard is very much like French in that it is not very hot. It is usually served with chips.

Μπέικον – μπ   *bacon*

Κοτόπουλο – τ   *chicken*

Καρότο – ρ   *carrot*

Παγωτό – ω   *ice cream*. Home-made Greek ice cream makes use of full-fat milk and cream and is very rich.

Unit 8

Στο – Σ   *at, in* or *on* depending on usage and context.

Μουσείο – ει   *museum*. Greek museums, despite the wealth of antiquities they have in storage, have been chronically underfunded. It is only in recent years that the government has begun to redress the balance. A lot of preservation work is being undertaken and more items are being put on display.

Δευτέρα – ευ   *Monday*. Literally translated, it means second day of the week.

Τρίτη – ρ   *Tuesday*, third day of the week.

Τετάρτη – η   *Wednesday*, fourth day of the week.

Πέμπτη – π   *Thursday*, fifth day of the week.

Παρασκευή – ευ   *Friday*. This means 'day of preparation'.

Σάββατο – β   *Saturday*, a word which bears more than a passing resemblance to the Sabbath.

Κυριακή – η   *Sunday*. Literally translated, it means the Lord's day.

Άκρη – ρ   *edge*

Πόλη – η   *town* or *city*. The word 'metropolitan' would not mean what it does today without the Greek word for 'city'.

Ποδήλατο – δ   *bicycle*

Βέσπα – B   a small motorcycle (taken from the Italian Vespa). Because they are cheap to obtain and run, and practical to use in the narrow streets of many Greek seaside towns and villages, small motorcycles like these have become a major source of noise pollution in recent years.

Τζιπ – τζ   *jeep*

Καράβι – ρ   *ship*

Τζατζίκι – τζ   a Greek garlic and yoghurt dip. Like many similar dishes, it originally came from the East and became part of Greek cuisine when Greece was a tiny part of the Ottoman Empire.

Αυγά – αυ   *eggs*. Battery farming is not yet in operation in Greece. Most eggs are produced, sold and bought locally, usually in open-air markets.

Ζάχαρη – Z   *sugar*

Βανίλια – B   *vanilla*

Αμερικάνικο – Α *American* (adjective)

Δολλάριο – Δ *dollar*

Αθήνα – θ *Athens*. The capital of Greece. Legend says that when Athens was built it was such a bright, vibrant city that the Olympian gods queued to become its patron. Of them all, Athena (The Goddess of Wisdom), and Poseidon (The God of the Ocean) won, and they each had to compete for the privilege. The contest was to give the city a gift to be judged by its elders. Poseidon was first and he struck the ground with his trident and made an eternal spring flow. Athena gave the city the olive tree. Of the two, hers was deemed to be the more valuable gift and the city was named after her, though Poseidon's spring still flows, and if you drink Athens water, legend states that you will always want to return to the city.

Μαδρίτη – η *Madrid*

Παρίσι – Π *Paris*

Ουάσινγκτον – ου *Washington DC*

Μεξικό – ξ *the city of Mexico*

Λονδίνο – Λ *London*

Unit 9

Ταξιδάκια – δ *small trips* or *excursions*. Quite a few Greek words use a special ending to make the word a 'diminutive', which slightly alters its meaning.

Δωδεκάνησα – Δ *Dodecanese* is the English form. Literally translated, it means 'twelve islands', because there were twelve islands in that group.

Δελφοί – οι Delphi. The famous temple of the oracle which was called the 'navel of the world' as it was thought to lie at the centre of the known world.

Σάμος – μ Samos, one of the Aegean Sea islands. It was one of the most important islands of the ancient world. Two of its most famous residents were Aesop, author of Aesop's Fables, and the mathematician Pythagoras.

Λαός – Λ   *people* or *crowd*

Λάδι – δ   *oil*, frequently *olive oil*. Most Greek cooking is done in olive oil.

Ωμέγα – Ω   *omega*. The final letter of the Greek alphabet.

Γκρίζο – Γκ   *grey*

Αγγούρι – γγ   *cucumber*. This is often used in Greek salads.

Άγγελος – γγ   *angel*. Directly from the Greek, we have borrowed the word 'angel', as well as 'archangel'.

Αγγίζω – ω   *I touch/I'm touching*

Άγγλος – γγ   *Englishman*

Ελευθεροτυπία – ευ   one more of the Athenian newspapers. It is now released as a national paper. A literal translation of the name means 'free press'.

Οικονομία – οι   *economy*

Πολιτική – η   *politics*. Greek politics is a very passionate, often polarizing, affair with the two main parties at the moment being left and right of centre.

Σπορ – Σ   *sport*. A word imported from English.

Πουλόβερ – ου   *pullover*

Δέκα – Δ   *ten*

Ευρώ – ευ   *euro*

Ρεκόρ – ρ   *record*

Κρήτη – η   *Crete*, the largest of the Greek islands and one with a history of rebellion. To date it is the only place in Greece where, despite the strict gun-control laws of the country, people openly carry guns and knives strapped to their belts.

Ελλάδα – λ   *Greece*

Αμοκ – κ *amok*. Another word which has been imported directly from the English.

Αγορές – γ *markets*

Unit 10

Σουβενίρ – Σ *souvenir*

Όμοιο – οι *the same, identical*

Φωνή – η *voice*. This is the reason the first record players were called 'phonographs' (writing in voice), and 'tele(afar) phone(voice)' also took its name from this word.

Ομόφωνη – η *homophone*

Χαρτί – χ *paper*

Χάρτης – Χ *map*

Βάζο – ζ *vase*

Βάζω – Ω *I put/I'm putting*

Κριτής – γ *judge*

Κρίνω – ω *I judge/I'm judging*

Κρίνος – ν *lily*

Φύλο – Φ *sex* (M and F)

Φίλος – λ *friend*

Χείρα – ει *hand* (formal Greek)

Χοίρα – οι *sow, female pig*

Χήρα – η *widow*

Άγαλμα – γ *statue*. Ancient Greeks actually believed that the more detailed a statue was, the closer to being alive it became. As a result they worked very hard on their statues to create detail which the world was not to see again until the opening years of the Renaissance.

Φωτογραφία – Φ *photograph*. Literally meaning 'writing in light'.

Μπλουζάκι – μπ *T-shirt*

Σημαία – αι *flag*. The Greek flag with its distinctive white and blue stripes and Greek cross is a code of the national anthem in Greece. The number of stripes on the flag is equal to the number of verses in the national anthem.

Εφημερίδα – Ε *newspaper*. Originally, newspapers in Greece were either government controlled or closely affiliated with a particular political party, which then financed them. This situation has now changed.

Εισιτήρια – ει *tickets*. It used to be that you could buy tickets on Greek buses from a conductor. In the mid 80s this changed, and you had to buy your ticket from a designated place, long before you boarded a bus. This created an interesting situation when it became apparent that the number of designated places selling bus tickets were few and far between. This situation has now, largely, been rectified and you can buy bus tickets from any street-corner kiosk.

Κασέτα – κ *cassette*

Τσάντα – τσ *handbag*

Θερμοκρασία – Θ *temperature*

Θερμόμετρο – μ *thermometer*, literally, nothing more than a 'counter' of temperature.

Όνομα – ο *name*. Greek names are usually taken from the Greek Orthodox calendar, which is the reason why, on certain islands which have a patron saint, a lot of people seem to have the same first name.

Ακρώνυμο – υ *acronym*

Ιχθύς – θ *fish*, but also the acronym by which Christians became known to each other, and Christianity became recognized.

Ιησούς – ου *Jesus*

Χριστός – τ *Christ*

Θεού – ου   *God's*

Υιός – ι   (formal) *son*

Σωτήρας – ω   *saviour*

Καλαματιανό – α   Greek dance from the area of Kalamata, a region also renowned for the quality of its olives and the richness of its olive oil.

Συρτάκι – κ   modern Greek dance. It became really popular during the early 1960s when a less athletic but equally communal dance to Καλαματιανό was being sought.

Κρητικός – η   As the name implies this is a Cretan dance, and like most Cretan dances is, essentially, a war dance. When performed by trained dancers, the lead dancer has a knife in one hand which he wields about as he jumps and gyrates through the air, held and aided by his second, who holds onto him by one end of a handkerchief.

Κλέφτικο – φ   a Greek dance dating back to the times when Greek rebels fought the Ottoman army.

Ρεμπέτικο – μπ   Unusually for a Greek dance, this is a solitary dance. Its roots are to be found in the Athens of the 1920s and 30s where the movement of the Ρεμπέτη got under way. Those who subscribed to it saw themselves as loners in a strange world, constantly fighting against the establishment through conscious non-conformity.

Δημοτικό – μ   a popular Greek dance which has many variations in different regions all over Greece. It is characterized by its upbeat, quick-step music and lively steps.

Ζελατίνα – Z   *jelly*

Καρτ-ποστάλ – ρ   *postcard*. This is an imported word from the French.

Ανάγραμμα – μ   *anagram*

Αίθριος – θ   *clement*, usually referring to weather

Άστατος – σ   *unsettled*

Συννεφιά – σ *heavy cloud*. Greece has 256 sun-drenched days a year!

Βροχή – Β *rain*. Most of the rainfall in Greece takes place during winter.

Καταιγίδα – κ *storm*

Χιόνι – χ *snow*. Even Greece experiences snowfall in winter, with some mountain villages being cut off for weeks on end. The botanical name for the early flowering small blue, pink or white bulb 'glory of the snow' is *chionodoxa*, from χιόνι + δόξα (glory).

Ομίχλη – χ *fog*

Χρήσιμες λέξεις
Useful words

We're almost there now. Your survival guide to the Greek alphabet, Greek culture and Greek way of life is almost complete. Below are some bits and pieces which you will find useful for reference. Dip in and out as necessary and don't be afraid to ask if you're not sure about the meaning of anything when in Greece.

It's a good sign – finding your way around

In most countries, everywhere you go you are bombarded by signs, and Greece is no exception. So that you will feel at home, and also perhaps avoid some potentially embarrassing situations, we have provided a list of some of the most common signs which you may meet or need.

ΓΥΝΑΙΚΩΝ	*LADIES*
ΑΝΔΡΩΝ	*GENTLEMEN*
ΚΙΝΔΥΝΟΣ	*DANGER*
ΣΤΑΣΙΣ	*STOP*
ΑΠΑΓΟΡΕΥΕΤΑΙ	*PROHIBITED, IT IS FORBIDDEN*
ΕΠΙΤΡΕΠΕΤΑΙ	*PERMITTED, IT IS ALLOWED*
ΑΝΟΙΚΤΟ	*OPEN*
ΚΛΕΙΣΤΟ	*CLOSED*
ΣΥΡΑΤΕ	*PULL*
ΩΘΗΣΑΤΕ	*PUSH*
ΕΙΣΟΔΟΣ	*ENTRANCE*
ΕΞΟΔΟΣ	*EXIT*
ΔΙΑΒΑΤΗΡΙΑ	*PASSPORTS*
ΤΟΥΑΛΕΤΑ	*TOILET*

Taking the lift

ΥΠΟΓ/ΥΠΟΓΕΙΟΝ	*BASEMENT*
ΙΣ/ΙΣΟΓΕΙΟΝ	*GROUND FLOOR*
ΗΜ/ΗΜΙΟΡΟΦΟΣ	*MEZZANINE FLOOR*
1ος	*1st floor*
2ος	*2nd floor*
3ος	*3rd floor*
4ος	*4th floor*

Forging good relationships

It isn't absolutely essential for you to remember these last two signs, but it would be very good for your εγώ, and give a boost to the cause of international friendship, to be able to recognize that

ΚΑΛΩΣΟΡΙΣΑΤΕ ΣΤΗΝ ΕΛΛΑΔΑ means *Welcome to Greece*
and
ΚΑΛΩΣΟΡΙΣΑΤΕ ΣΤΗΝ ΚΥΠΡΟ means *Welcome to Cyprus*.

It all adds up – Greek numbers

0	μηδέν	11	έντεκα
1	ένα	12	δώδεκα
2	δύο	13	δεκατρία
3	τρεις	14	δεκατέσσερα
4	τέσσερεις	15	δεκαπέντε
5	πέντε	16	δεκαέξι
6	έξι	17	δεκαεφτά
7	εφτά or επτά	18	δεκαοχτώ
8	οχτώ or οκτώ	19	δεκαεννιά
9	εννιά or εννέα	20	είκοσι
10	δέκα	21	είκοσι ένα

22	είκοσι δύο	26	είκοσι έξι
23	είκοσι τρία	27	είκοσι εφτά
24	είκοσι τέσσερα	28	είκοσι οχτώ
25	είκοσι πέντε	29	είκοσι εννιά

You have already met the two ways of writing the Greek for seven, eight and nine, and you can use either version whenever these digits crop up. Twenty-seven, for example can be either είκοσι εφτά or είκοσι επτά.

There are several other numbers that for grammatical reasons have more than one form in Greek, but we aren't proposing to confuse you by giving them here. If, as we hope, our introduction to Greek script has shown you that the alphabet is nowhere near as hard as it's cracked up to be, we are fairly confident that you'll take our word for it when we say that if you go on to learn more Greek, you'll soon know which form to use, and anyway, everyone will understand you, even if you use the wrong one by mistake.

30	τριάντα	70	εβδομήντα
40	σαράντα	80	ογδόντα
50	πενήντα	90	ενενήντα
60	εξήντα		

To make the numbers 31–99, follow the same pattern as shown for 21–29, substituting the appropriate digits.

100 εκατό (Note that in English we say '*one* hundred' but in Greek you leave out the 'one'.)

Just when you thought that you were getting the hang of this, some ancient Greek mathematician had to come along and complicate things! If you want to use 200, 300 or any of the hundreds up to and including 900, the word for hundred changes to -κοσια. The preceding word also changes slightly, but is still recognizable. If you forget, for example, that it's εξακόσια and not έξι-κοσια when you collect the key at the hotel, you will (probably!) still end up in the right room.

200	διακόσια
300	τριακόσια
400	τετρακόσια
500	πεντακόσια
600	εξακόσια
700	εφτακόσια
800	οχτακόσια
900	εννιακόσια

Thousands are much easier to manage. Mike and Lisa introduced you to χίλια (thousand) and χιλιάδες (thousands) so all you do is combine words that you already know how to make.

1000	χίλια (once again, it's just 'thousand' not '*one* thousand')
2000	δύο χιλιάδες
3000	τρείς χιλιάδες
4000	τέσσερεις χιλιάδες
5000	πέντε χιλιάδες
6000	έξι χιλιάδες
7000	εφτά χιλιάδες
8000	οχτώ χιλιάδες
9000	εννιά χιλιάδες
1 000 000	ένα εκατομμύριο

We could go on forever of course, but you probably have enough numbers here to keep you going for a while!

Keeping track of time the Greek way

Greeks have a peculiar notion of time. Morning (πρωί) in Greece starts pretty much about the same time as it does everywhere else in the world, but noon (μεσημέρι) does not really start until about 1 p.m. and it goes on until 4 p.m. As soon as you get past the 4 p.m. watershed, afternoon takes over and this lasts until sundown (which varies slightly depending on the time of year) and then you have night (βράδυ or νύχτα). While Greeks are perfectly well aware of this arrangement, many visitors to the country are not. Greeks don't know this. Arrange to meet in a local in the 'afternoon' without naming a precise time and you could be in for a lengthy wait.

Days of the week

Κυριακή	Sunday	**Πέμπτη**	Thursday
Δευτέρα	Monday	**Παρασκευή**	Friday
Τρίτη	Tuesday	**Σαββάτο**	Saturday
Τετάρη	Wednesday		

Months of the year

Ιανουάριος	January	**Ιούλιος**	July
Φεβρουάριος	February	**Αύγουστος**	August
Μάρτιος	March	**Σεπτέμβριος**	September
Απρίλιος	April	**Οκτώβριος**	October
Μάιος	May	**Νοέμβριος**	November
Ιούνιος	June	**Δεκέμβριος**	December

Seasons

άνοιξη	spring	**φθινόπωρο**	autumn
καλοκαίρι	summer	**χειμώνας**	winter

The four corners of the earth

βορράς	north	**ανατολή**	east
νότος	south	**δύση**	west

Relationships

Greeks believe in extended families and many live very close to their relatives. Some of the terms used to describe family relationships are probably familiar; some, however, will be strange enough to require a little attention.

πατέρας	*father*	εξάδελφος	*cousin* (male)
μητέρα	*mother*	εξαδέλφη	*cousin* (female)
γονιός	*parent*	παππούς	*grandfather*
γονείς	*parents*	γιαγιά	*grandmother*
αδελφός	*brother*	εγγονός	*grandson*
αδελφή	*sister*	εγγονή	*granddaughter*

A brief history of Ancient Greece

'The glory that was Greece', in the words of Edgar Allan Poe, was short-lived and confined to a very small geographic area. Yet, thanks to the development of the Byzantine Empire, which succeeded it, and its absorption by the Roman Empire, which conquered it, it has influenced the growth of Western civilization far out of proportion to its size and duration.

These three pillars are all that remain of a temple to Apollo erected by the Spartans in 625 BC to thank the Oracle for her reading of what they should do in the war against the Athenians. The Spartans paid great heed to omens and the readings of the Oracle and would rarely start a campaign or fight a battle without sending for a reading. The temple itself was destroyed by floods and earthquakes some 200 years later.

The Greece that Poe praised was primarily Athens during its Golden Age in the 5th century BC. Strictly speaking, the state was Attica; Athens was its heart. The English poet John Milton called Athens 'the eye of Greece, mother of arts and eloquence'. Athens was the city-state in which the arts, philosophy and democracy flourished. At least it was the city that attracted those who wanted to work, speak and think in an environment of freedom. In the rarefied atmosphere of Athens, were born ideas about human nature and political society that are fundamental to the Western world today.

Athens may have been the brightest of its city-states but it was not the whole of Greece. Sparta, Corinth, Thebes and Thessalonica were but a few of the many other city-states that existed on the rocky and mountainous peninsula at the southern end of the Balkans. Each city-state was an independent political unit, and each vied with the others for power and wealth. These city-states planted Greek colonies in Asia Minor, on many islands in the Aegean Sea, and in southern Italy and Sicily.

The story of Ancient Greece began between 1900 and 1600 BC. At that time the Greeks – or Hellenes, as they called themselves – were simple nomadic herdsmen. Their language shows that they were a branch of the Indo–European-speaking peoples. They came from the grasslands east of the Caspian Sea, driving their flocks and herds before them. They entered the peninsula from the north, one small group after another.

The first invaders were the blue-eyed, fair-haired Achaeans of whom Homer wrote. The dark-haired, stockier but war-like Dorians came perhaps three or four centuries later and subjugated the Achaean tribes. Other tribes, the Aeolians and the Ionians, found homes chiefly on the islands in the Aegean Sea and on the coast of Asia Minor.

The land that these tribes invaded – the Aegean Basin – was the site of a well-developed Aegean civilization. The people who lived there had cities and palaces. They used gold and bronze and made pottery and paintings.

The Greek invaders were still in the barbarian stage. They plundered and destroyed the Aegean cities. Gradually, as they settled and intermarried with the people they conquered, they absorbed some of the Aegean culture.

Little is known of the earliest stages of Greek settlement. The invaders probably moved southward from their pasturelands along the Danube, bringing their families and primitive goods in rough oxcarts. Along the way they grazed their herds. In the spring they stopped long enough to plant and harvest a single crop. Gradually they settled down to form communities ruled by kings and elders.

The background of the two great Greek epics – the *Iliad* and the *Odyssey* – is the background of the Age of Kings. These epics depict the simple, warlike life of the early Greeks. The Achaeans had excellent weapons and sang stirring songs. Such luxuries as they possessed, however – gorgeous robes, jewellery, elaborate metalwork – they bought from the Phoenician traders.

The *Iliad* tells how Greeks from many city-states – among them, Sparta, Athens, Thebes, and Argos – joined forces to fight their common foe, Troy in Asia Minor. In historical times the Greek city-states were again able to combine when the power of Persia threatened them. However, this diversity, which produced the cultural wealth of Ancient Greece, was also its curse, for it never became a nation. The only patriotism the Ancient Greek knew was loyalty to his city. The size of each city-state, at the time, did not make for much more than 10,000 people. Athens was probably the only Greek city-state with more than 20,000 citizens and it ruled mostly by its size and glitter; its gravity in the affairs of the city-states around it was counterbalanced by the military might of Sparta.

Only in a few cases did a city-state push its holdings beyond very narrow limits. Athens held the whole plain of Attica, and most of the Attic villagers were Athenian citizens. Argos conquered the plain of Argolis. Sparta made a conquest of Laconia and part of the fertile plain of Messenia. The conquered people were subjects, not citizens. Thebes attempted to be the ruling city of Boeotia but never quite succeeded.

Similar city-states were found all over the Greek world, which had flung its outposts throughout the Aegean Basin and even beyond. There were Greeks in all the islands of the Aegean. Among these islands was Thasos, famous for its gold mines. Samothrace, Imbros, and Lemnos were long occupied by Athenian colonists. Other Aegean islands colonized by Greeks included Lesbos, the home of the poet Sappho; Scyros, the island of Achilles; and Chios, Samos and Rhodes. Also settled by Greeks were the nearer-lying Cyclades – so called (from the Greek word for 'circle') because they encircled the sacred island of Delos – and the southern island of Crete.

The western shores of Asia Minor were fringed with Greek colonies, reaching out past the Propontis (Sea of Marmara) and the Bosphorus to the northern and southern shores of the Euxine, or Black Sea. In Africa there were, among others, the colony of Cyrene, now the site of a town in Libya, and the trading post of Naucratis in Egypt. Sicily too was colonized by the Greeks, and there and in southern Italy so many colonies were planted that this region came to be known as Magna Graecia (Great Greece). Pressing farther still, the Greeks founded the city of Massilia, now Marseilles, France.

Separated by barriers of sea and mountain, by local pride and jealousy, the various independent city-states never conceived the idea of uniting the Greek-speaking world into a single political unit. They formed alliances only when some powerful city-state embarked on a career of conquest and attempted to make itself leader of the rest. Many influences made for unity – a common language, a common religion, a common literature, similar customs, the religious leagues and festivals, the Olympic Games – but even in time of foreign invasion it was difficult to induce the cities to act together, a fact which they were to regret in later times, when other, more powerful, invaders cast their eyes towards the glitter that was Greece, and decided that the time had come to make her theirs.

If the Greek language is as complex and as beautiful as it is today, it owes a lot to this tumultuous history. It is to the discipline-loving Spartans for example that we owe the sense of the austere (hence the word Spartan). Similarly the Delphic Oracle of Pythia with her cryptic replies gave us the word 'pithy' for a short, to-the-point phrase.

Similarly, the Greek alphabet you have been studying bears traces of the history it has passed through. The difference in sounds, the funny-looking letters and the letter combinations to make different sounds, all betray the Egyptian and Phoenician influence of the past. They show traces of Byzantinian dabbling and reveal, at times, the subtlety that made Byzantinian politics the deadly power game it was.

To study the alphabet of any language is to launch oneself upon a tide of history and feel the beauty of the past. It is also but the first step in a journey which is just beginning.

Επίλογος
Epilogue

We entered this book with the prologue (from the thoroughly Greek word πρόλογος, προ = 'before' + λόγος = 'word'), so we now have to make our exit with the equally Greek επίλογος (επι = 'on top of' / 'in addition'). By now, reading or writing the Greek alphabet will be a piece of cake, and you may want to start finding out more for yourself, instead of relying on us to choose what you are going to learn. This means that, even if you haven't already done so, you'll soon need to use a dictionary. As you've probably noticed, Greek alphabetical order is slightly different from that of English, and this can make using a dictionary frustrating until you get used to its idiosyncrasies, or ιδιοσυγκρασίες, as the Greek would say. It is, for example, somewhat disconcerting for the English speaker to find Z popping up next to E in a Greek dictionary.

To help you, we've provided some exercises which give you a chance to practise Greek alphabetical order. Most words in Greek dictionaries are written in lower-case letters, so there are many occasions when you will have to switch from capitals to lower case if you want to look them up. The words you find on road signs, in cartoons or newspaper headlines, for instance, are usually written in capitals. But first of all, here is the Greek alphabet again, below, with the letter names written alongside. You don't have to learn the names in order to use a dictionary, but you may find that it helps you to remember the order when you are looking up a word, if you can mutter the letters as you go along. As you can see, there are a few letters where the handwritten forms tend to be slightly different from the printed version. Also, note that the Greek ι, unlike its English counterpart, is not dotted. If you write the English form, *i*, the dot could be mistaken for a stress mark.

THE GREEK ALPHABET			
PRONUNCIATION	CAPITALS	LOWER CASE	HANDWRITTEN FORM
alpha	A	α	α
vita	B	β	β
ghama	Γ	γ	γ
thelta	Δ	δ	δ
epsilon	E	ε	ε
zita	Z	ζ	ζ
ita	H	η	η
thita	Θ	θ	θ
yota	I	ι	ι
kapa	K	κ	κ
lamda	Λ	λ	λ
mi	M	μ	μ
ni	N	ν	ν
xi	Ξ	ξ	ξ
omikron	O	o	o
pi	Π	π	π
rho	P	ρ	ρ
sigma	Σ	σ, ς	σ
taf	T	τ	τ
ipsilon	Υ	υ	υ
fi	Φ	φ	φ
hi	X	χ	χ
psi	Ψ	ψ	ψ
omega	Ω	ω	ω

Exercise 1

Fill in the missing letters of each sequence.

1 α – γ – ε – η – ι – λ – ν – ο – ρ – τ – φ – ψ –

2 – β – δ – ζ – θ – κ – μ – ξ – π – σ – υ – χ – ω

Now try to write out the Greek alphabet in lower-case letters from α to θ. As soon as you can do that, try going a little further – maybe as far as π. Keep adding a few letters until you can make it all the way to ω. With that skill safely under your belt, repeat the process using capital letters.

Exercise 2

1 Α – Γ – Ε – Η – Ι – Λ – Ν – Ο – Ρ – Τ – Φ – Ψ –

2 – Β – Δ – Ζ – Θ – Κ – Μ – Ξ – Π – Σ – Υ – Χ – Ω

Impress your friends!

If you have access to a computer, you can show off by signing your name in Greek characters every time you send an e-mail. The 'symbol' font in many computers changes the English letters on the keyboard to their Greek equivalents. Where there is no exact counterpart 'symbol' uses spare English letters.

The English *U* becomes the Greek **θ**, you press *H* for **η**, the English *y* is used for **ψ**, and you press *v* when you need **ω**.

Using a street map

A word that you will meet all the time is ΟΔΟΣ = STREET. In England you might find King Street, but in Greece, ΟΔΟΣ comes first, and it becomes 'Street of the King'. Greek grammar changes the ending of King, but this shouldn't put you off striking out on your own to that little taverna that hardly anyone knows about, where they serve the most marvellous … but that would be telling! You'll just have to go and find out for yourself!

Using a dictionary

By now you have enough knowledge to be able to look up most of the words which you will meet on that idyllic trip to Greece, which we hope that you are planning. You may find, however, that, as in English, the word in the dictionary is not exactly the same as the one you want. In English, for example, you won't find 'eaten' as a separate entry, although you will find 'eat'. This shouldn't be too much of a problem because it's usually the endings that may change for most of the words that you'll need to look up at this stage, so you'll probably be able to work out the meaning. We firmly believe that a dictionary is a journey rather than a destination. We hope you enjoy yours.

Λεξικό
Dictionary

A α

άγαλμα   *statue*
άγγελος   *angel*. It is also a Greek name, though less common now.
αγγίζω   *I touch / I'm touching*
Άγγλος   *Englishman*
αγορά   *market*. Also a buy as in 'I've made a buy' έκανα μία αγορά.
αγοράζω   *I buy / I'm buying*
αγορές   *markets*
αγγούρι   *cucumber*

άγουρο   *unripe*. Used for fruit and vegetables.
αεροπλάνο   *aeroplane*
Αθήνα   *Athens*
αίθριος   *clement*, usually referring to weather.
άκρη   *edge*
ακρώνυμο   *acronym*
Ακρόπολη   an influential Athenian daily paper. Also the 'edge' of a city; its highest part. Every ancient Greek city had an acropolis, though the one most famous now is the one in Athens.
αλάτι   *salt*, also seen as αλας on some packets of salt.
Αμερικάνικο   *American* (adjective)
Αμερική   *America*
αμοκ   *amok*
ανάγραμμα   *anagram*
Απογευματινή   initially a daily newspaper appearing only in Athens (as most papers did at the time), it's now a national paper.
αρτοπωλείο   *bakery*
άρτος   bread. Old Greek.
ασπιρίνη   *aspirin*. This is a compound word for white (άσπρη) and fiery (πυρίνη).
άστατος   *unsettled*
ακατάστατος   *untidy*
άτομο   *atom, individual*
αυγά   *eggs*
Αυστραλία   *Australia*
αυτοκίνητο   *car*

Β β

βάζο   *vase*
βάζω   *I put / I'm putting*
βανίλια   *vanilla*
Βέσπα   *small motorcycle* or *Vespa*
βιβλίο (βιβλία)   *book(s)*
βιβλιοπωλείο   *bookshop*
βούτυρο   *butter*
βροχή   *rain*

Γ γ

γάλα *milk*

γαλακτοπωλείο shop selling only dairy produce such as eggs, milk and **yoghurt**.

γεμιστά *stuffed tomatoes* (usually)

για *for, about*

γιαούρτι *yoghurt*. Greek yoghurt is usually made from either sheep's or goat's milk.

γιατί *why, because*

γκρίζο *grey*

γλυκά *sweets* (plural)

γλυκό *sweet*

γράμμα *letter*, both a letter of the alphabet and a letter one can post.

γραμματόσημα *stamps*

Δ δ

δέκα ten

δεκαεννέα *nineteen*, pronounced as δεκαεννέα or δεκαεννιά.

δεκαέξι *sixteen*

δεκαεπτά *seventeen*. Again, this one may be pronounced and written as either δεκαεπτά or δεκαεφτά

δεκαοκτώ *eighteen*, pronounced either as δεκαοκτώ or δεκαοχτώ

Δελφοί *Delphi*, famous oracle of Apollo.

δέμα *parcel, packet*

δεν *not*

δεξιά *right*

Δευτέρα *Monday*. In Greek it literally means the second day of the week.

Δημοτικό a Greek dance. It means popular or of the people. There are several regional types of 'popular' dances which come from different parts of Greece.

διαμέρισμα *flat, apartment*

δολλάριο *dollar*

δραχμή the old Greek currency

δρόμος *road*

δύο *two*
δώδεκα *twelve*
δωδεκάνησα *Dodecanese*
δωμάτιο *room*

Ε ε

εδώ *here*
εισιτήρια *tickets*
είσοδος *entrance*
εκατό *a hundred*
έλεος *mercy*
Ελευθεροτυπία one more of the Athenian newspapers
έλικας *rotor blades*
ελικόπτερο *helicopter*
Ελλάδα *Greece*
Ελληνικός (Ελληνική, Ελληνικό) *Greek*. It is also the name by which Greek coffee, a potent brew, is known.
ένα *one*
εννέα *nine*. Its alternative is εννιά.
έξι *six*
έξω *out*
επάνω *up* (older form of πανω)
επίλογος *epilogue*. The last word, or conclusion of a work or play.
επτά *seven*, or, alternatively, εφτά.
εστιατόριο *restaurant*
ευγένεια *politeness*, also nobility.
ευγενής *noble, polite*
ευγενικός *polite*
εύκολο *easy*
ευρώ *Euro*
ευχαριστώ *thank you*
εφημερίδα *newspaper*

Ζ ζ

ζάχαρη *sugar*
ζαχαροπλαστείο *pâtisserie*
ζελατίνα *jelly*

ζέστη *heat*
ζεστός *hot*

Η η

ηλιοθεραπεία *sunbathing*
ήλιος *the sun*

Θ θ

θέλω *I want*
Θεού *God's*
θερμό *a thermos flask*
θερμός *warm*
Θερμοκρασία *temperature*
θερμόμετρο *thermometer*

Ι ι

Ιαπωνία *Japan*
ιδέα *idea*
Ιταλία *Italy*
Ιησούς *Jesus*
ιχθύς *fish*

Κ κ

καδένα *neck* or *watch chain*, usually made of gold.
καζάνι *cauldron*
και *and*
κακό *bad*
Καλαματιανό Greek dance from the area of Kalamata.
κάνω *I do, I make / I'm doing, I'm making*
καράβι *ship*
καρότο *carrot*
καρπούζι *water melon*
καρτ-ποστάλ *postcard*
κασέτα *cassette*
καταιγίδα *storm*

κάτω   *down*

καφέ   *coffee, brown*

καφέδες   *coffees*

καφενείο   the more traditional type of coffee shop. A *kafenio* is a very old concept. It is a predominantly men-only environment, and each has its own catchment area, much as a local pub in England would. It is not unusual for Greek men to spend all day in a *kafenio*, drinking ouzo and playing backgammon.

καφετερία   *a coffee shop*

κετσάπ   *ketchup*

κεφτεδάκια   *small meatballs*

κεφτέδες   *meatballs*

κεφτές   *meatball.* Also used as a derogatory word, i.e. to say someone is a 'meatball' is the equivalent of a 'butter-fingers' or also a 'mummy's boy'.

κινηματογράφος   *cinema.* Literally translated, it means, 'writing in motion'.

κίνηση   *movement*, as in motion. Also used to describe road traffic.

κίνημα   *movement*, as in political faction.

κινητό   *mobile.* Particularly useful when combined with the word 'phone'.

Κλέφτικο   a Greek dance

κόμμα   *comma* (the punctuation mark)

Κορέα   *Korea*

κοτόπουλο   *chicken*

κρασί   *wine*

Κρήτη   *Crete*

Κρητικός   a Cretan dance

κρίνος   *lily*

κρίνω   *I judge / I'm judging*

κριτής   *judge, critic*

Κυριακή   *Sunday.* Literally translated, it means the Lord's day.

Λ λ

λάδι   *oil.* The term is applied equally to olive oil, sun-tan oil and motor oil.

λαός   *people massed together*, and *race*, as in race of people.

λεμονάδα *lemonade*
λεμόνια *lemons*
λεωφορείο *bus*
Λονδίνο *London*

Μ μ

μαγαζί *shop*. This is applied in a generic manner to any shop in Greece.
Μαδρίτη *Madrid*
μακαρονάδα *cooked spaghetti*
μάξι *a long skirt*. The opposite of a mini skirt.
μαρούλι *lettuce*
μαρτίνι *martini*
με *with*
μεγάλα *plural, big, large*
μεγάλος *big, large, old*
μεζές *tit bit*
μενού *menu*
Μεσημβρινή originally an Athenian newspaper, now national (lit. noon paper). Others like it are: Σημεριανή (Today's paper), Κήρυκας (translated as the perhaps slightly ambitious 'Gospel') and Εθνική (National).
Μεξικό *Mexico City*
μήλα *apples*
μηλόπιττα *apple pie*
μικρά *small, little* (plural)
μίνι *mini* literally, the British cult car, but also a short skirt.
μόνο *alone, only*
μοσχαρίσια *beef*
μουσείο *museum*
μουστάρδα *mustard*
μπαρ *bar*. This is another imported word.
μπέικον *bacon*
μπισκότα *biscuits*
μπλουζάκι *t-shirt*
μπουκάλι *bottle*
μπουκάλια *bottles*
μπριζόλα *steak*

μπύρα *beer*
μπυραρία where you would go to drink beer and have a meze.

N ν

νερό *water.* The plural is νερα!
νότα *a musical note*
ντεντέκτιβ *detective*
ντισκοτέκ *disco*
ντομάτες *tomatoes*

Ξ ξ

ξενοδοχείο *hotel*
ξένος *foreigner, stranger*

Ο ο

οδός *street*
οικονομία *economy*
οκταπόδι *octopus.* It may also be spelled as οχταπόδι and
   sometimes it's pronounced in the contracted form of χταπόδι. On
   menus it may appear in its diminutive of χταποδάκια (small octopi)
οκτώ *eight.* This can be pronounced as either οκτώ or οχτώ.
όλα *all, everything*
ομελέτα *omelette*
ομίχλη *fog*
όμοιο *the same, identical*
ομόφωνη *homophone*
όνομα *name*
οπωροπωλείο *a fruit shop*
Ουάσινγκτον *Washington DC*
ουζερί a specialist outlet, traditionally cheap, where sailors and
   villagers would congregate to drink ouzo and listen to live music
   played on a mandolin.
ούζο the clear-coloured, fiery Greek drink which goes milky
   when water is added to it.
ουίσκυ *whisky*

Π π

πάγος *ice*
παγωτό *ice cream*
πακέτο *packet, parcel*
πάνω *up*
παρακαλώ *please*
παρασκευή *Friday*. The word means 'day of preparation'.
Παρίσι *Paris*
παστίτσιο a pasta and mincemeat dish whose origins lie more in the East than Greece.
πατατάκια *crisps*
πατάτες *potatoes, chips*
πάω *I go / I'm going*
Πελοπόννησος a regional newspaper. As the name suggests it is limited to the Peloponnese area.
Πέμπτη *Thursday*. Fifth day of the week.
πίνω *I drink / I'm drinking*
πιπέρι *pepper*
πίτσα *pizza*
πιτσαρία the place where you would expect to buy a pizza
πόλη *town, city*
ποδήλατο *bicycle*
πολιτική *politics*
πολύ *very, a lot*
πορτοκαλάδα *orangeade*
πορτοκάλι *orange*
ποτό *drink*
πούλμαν *coach*
πουλόβερ *pullover, sweater*

Ρ ρ

ρεκόρ *record* (in sport, for example, rather than music)
Ρεμπέτικο a Greek dance. The favourite of those who suffer from a 'heavy heart', *rebetika* are usually songs about abandonment and unfulfilment, and are accompanied by the mournful sound of the mandolin.

ρετσίνα the famous Greek wine, which takes its name from the resin now used to flavour it.

Ρώσικο Ρούβλι *the Russian rouble*

Σ σ

Σάββατο *Saturday*

σαγανάκι traditionally ouzeri food. It consists of fried hard cheese and fried squid or octopus served in a light vinaigrette dressing.

σαλάτα *salad*

Σάμος the island of *Samos*

σάντουιτς *sandwich*. The concept of the sandwich is relatively new in Greek culture and still considered something of a novelty in certain remote parts.

σήμα *sign, badge, signal*

σημαία *flag*

σιδηρόδρομος *railway*

σίδηρος *iron*

σοκ *shock*. This is an imported word into Greek.

σοκολάτα *chocolate*

σουβενίρ *souvenir*

σοφία *wisdom*. The old Greek church (now a mosque) in Istanbul is called *Agia Sofia* (Holy Wisdom).

σπορ *sport*

στο *at, in,* or *on*, depending on usage and context.

συμπεριφορά *behaviour*

συννεφιά *heavy cloud*

Συρτάκι a modern Greek dance

σως *sauce*. Usually refers to tomato sauce.

σωτήρας *saviour*

Τ τ

ταβέρνα a traditional Greek restaurant

ταξί *taxi*

ταξιδάκια *small trips* or *excursions*

τανξ *tank*

ταχυδρομείο *post office*

τελεφερίκ *cable car*
Τετάρτη *Wednesday*. Fourth day of the week.
τζατζίκι a Greek garlic and yoghurt dip.
τζιπ *jeep*. In Greek this refers generically to most four-wheel-drive vehicles.
τηγανητές *fried* (usually refers to chips).
τεκίλα *tequila*
τομή *a cut*, usually along a premarked line
τόξο *bow* (as in 'bow and arrow')
τραίνο *train*
τριμμένο *grated*
Τρίτη *Tuesday*. Third day of the week.
τρόποι *manners, method, way*
τρόποι συμπεριφοράς *manners* (literally 'way of behaviour')
τρώμε *we eat / we are eating*
τσάντα *handbag*
τυρί *cheese*
τυροπωλείο a shop specializing in the sale of cheese

Υ υ

υιός *son* (formal Greek)
υποβρύχιο *submarine*

Φ φ

φαγητό *food*
φαρμακείο *pharmacy, chemist's*
φαστ φουντ *fast food*
φεριμπότ *ferry* (boat)
φέτα a soft, white Greek cheese, made out of goat's milk, with a distinctive flavour and texture.
φίλη *a female friend*
φιλμ *movie, film*
φίλος *a masculine friend*
φορτηγό *truck*
φούρνου *oven baked*. Quite a lot of food is cooked this way in Greece.
φρούτα *fruit*

φρουτοπωλείο   a place where you would go to buy fresh fruit and vegetables.

φύλο   *sex* (M and F)

φωνή   *voice*

φωτογραφία   *photograph*

Χ χ

χάμπουρκερ   *hamburger*

χάρτης   *map*

χαρτί   *paper*

χείρα   *hand* (formal)

χήρα   *widow*

χίλια   *a thousand*

χιόνι   *snow*

χοίρα   *sow* (female pig)

χοιρινή   *pork*

χορός   *dance*

χωριάτικη   usually known as Greek salad, though the more literal translation is 'village salad'

Χριστός   *Christ*

χρυσός   *gold*

χρυσοχοείο   *jeweller's*

χρυσόψαρο   *goldfish*

χρυσοθήρας   *gold digger*

Ψ ψ

ψάρι   *fish*

ψαροπωλείο   *a fishmonger's*

ψωμί   *bread*

ψώνια   *the shopping*

ψωνίζω   *I buy / I am buying*

Ω ω

ωμέγα   *omega*, the final letter of the Greek alphabet.

ώρα   *time*

ωραία   *nice*

English–Greek vocabulary

about για
acronym ακρώνυμο
acropolis Ακρόπολη
aeroplane αεροπλάνο
afternoon απόγευμα
alone μόνο
America Αμερική
American Αμερικάνικο
(An American person is either
Αμερικανός (m.) or
Αμερικανίδα (f.))
amok αμοκ
anagram ανάγραμμα
and και
angel άγγελος
apple pie μηλόπιττα
apples μήλα
aspirin ασπιρίνη
at (the) στο
Athens Αθήνα
atom άτομο
Australia Αυστραλία

bacon μπέικον
bad κακό
badge σήμα
baked φούρνου
bakery αρτοπωλείο
bar μπαρ
because γιατί
beef μοσχαρίσια
beer μπύρα
behaviour συμπεριφορά

bicycle ποδήλατο
big μεγάλος (s.) μεγάλα (pl.)
biscuits μπισκότα
book βιβλίο
bookshop βιβλιοπωλείο
bottle μπουκάλι
bottles μπουκάλια
bow (as in bow and arrow) τόξο
bread άρτος (old Greek),
ψωμι
brown καφέ
bus λεωφορείο
butter βούτυρο
buy: I am buying = ψωνίζω,
αγοράζω (Also 'a buy' as in
'I've made a buy' έκανα μια
αγορά)

cable car τελεφερίκ
car αυτοκίνητο
carrot καρότο
cassette κασέτα
cauldron καζάνι
cheese τυρί
chicken κοτόπουλο
chips πατάτες
chocolate σοκολάτα
Christ Χριστός
cinema κινηματογράφος
clement (weather) αίθριος
cloud συννεφιά
coach πούλμαν
coffee καφέ

coffee shop καφετερία (The more traditional type of coffee shop is a καφενείο)
coffees καφέδες
comma κόμμα
Crete Κρήτη
crisps πατατάκια
cucumber αγγούρι
cut (noun), usually along a pre-marked line τομή

dairy, i.e. a shop selling only dairy produce γαλακτοπωλείο
dance χορός
Delphi, famous oracle of Apollo Δελφοί
detective ντέντεκτιβ
disco ντισκοτέκ
do: I'm doing = κάνω
Dodecanese Δωδεκάνησα. Greek islands of the Aegean (literally, twelve islands, although only the major ones have a permanent population and some of the smaller ones are used only for fishing or keeping sheep on)
dollar δολλάριο
down κάτω
drachma δραχμή
drink ποτό I'm drinking πίνω

easy εύκολο
eat: we are eating = τρώμε
economy οικονομία
edge άκρη
eggs αυγά
eight οκτώ, οχτώ

eighteen δεκαοκτώ, δεκαοχτώ
Englishman Άγγλος
entrance είσοδος
epilogue επίλογος
Euro ευρώ
excursions ταξιδάκια
exit έξοδος

fast food φαστ φουντ
ferry boat φεριμπότ
fiery πύρινη
fish ιχθύς, ψάρι
fishmonger's ψαροπωλείο
flag σημαία
fog ομίχλη
food φαγητό
for για
foreigner ξένος
Friday Παρασκευή
fried (usually refers to chips) τηγανητές
friend φίλος (m.), φίλη (f.)
fruit φρούτα
fruit shop οπωροπωλείο

God's, of God Θεού
go: I'm going = πάω
gold χρυσός
gold digger χρυσοθήρας
goldfish χρυσόψαρο
Greece Ελλάδα
Greek (adj.) Ελληνικός (a Greek person is Έλληνας (m.) or Ελληνίδα (f.))
grey γκρίζο

hamburger χάμπουρκερ
handbag τσάντα

heat ζέστη
helicopter ελικόπτερο
here εδώ
homophone ομόφωνη
hot ζεστό
hotel ξενοδοχείο
hundred εκατό

ice πάγος
ice cream παγωτό
idea ιδέα
identical όμοιο
important μεγάλος (s.),
  μεγάλα (pl.)
in (the) στο
individual άτομο
iron σίδηρο
Italian Ιταλική
Italy Ιταλία

Japan Ιαπωνία
jeep τζιπ
jelly ζελατίνα
Jesus Ιησούς
jeweller's (shop) χρυσοχοείο
judge, critic κριτής
judge: I'm judging = κρίνω

ketchup κέτσαπ
Korea Κορέα

lemonade λεμονάδα
lemons λεμόνια
letter (both a letter of the
  alphabet and a letter one can
  post) γράμμα
lettuce μαρούλι
lily κρίνος

London Λονδίνο
lot, many πολύ

Madrid Μαδρίτη
make: I'm making = κάνω
manners (literally, way
  of behaviour) τρόποι
  συμπεριφοράς
map χάρτης
market αγορά
markets αγορές
martini μαρτίνι
maxi μάξι
meatballs κεφτέδες (small
  meatballs are κεφτεδάκια.)
menu μενού
mercy έλεος
method τρόποι
Mexico Μεξικό
milk γάλα
mini (the British cult car or a
  short skirt) μίνι
mobile κινητό (particularly
  useful when combined with
  the word τηλέφωνο 'phone')
Monday Δευτέρα
movement (political faction)
  κινημα, (road traffic) κίνηση
movie, film φιλμ
museum μουσείο
mustard μουστάρδα

name όνομα
neck chain, usually made of
  gold καδένα
newspaper εφημερίδα
nine εννέα, εννιά
nineteen δεκαεννέα, δεκαεννιά

nobility ευγένεια
noble ευγενής
not δεν
note (musical) νότα

octopus οκταπόδι, οχταπόδι, χταποδάκια (small octopi)
oil λάδι
old μεγάλος
omega, the final letter of the Greek alphabet ωμέγα (Also used as a symbol for the last word in anything, for example, the Omega theory in cosmology about the end of time and omega particles in physics which are the final products of experiments in cyclotrons (particle accelerators))
omelette ομελέτα
on (the) στο
one ένα
only μόνο
orange πορτοκάλι
orangeade πορτοκαλάδα
out έξω
ouzo ούζο
oven φούρνος

packet πακέτο, δέμα
paper χαρτί
parcel πακέτο, δέμα
Paris Παρίσι
pâtisserie ζαχαροπλαστείο
people (race) λαός
pepper πιπέρι
pharmacy, chemist's φαρμακείο

photograph φωτογραφία
pizza πίτσα
please παρακαλώ
polite ευγενικός, ευγενής
politeness ευγένεια (literally, nobility)
politics πολιτική
pork χοιρινή
postcard καρτ-ποστάλ
post office ταχυδρομείο
potatoes πατάτες
pullover πουλόβερ
put: I'm putting = βάζω

race (of people) λαός
railway σιδηρόδρομος
record (for example, in sport) ρεκόρ
restaurant εστιατόριο
retsina ρετσίνα
right δεξιά
road δρόμος
room δωμάτιο
rotor blades έλικας
Rouble Ρούβλι

salad σαλάτα
salt αλάτι, άλας
same όμοιο
Samos Σάμος
sandwich σάντουιτς
Saturday Σάββατο
sauce (usually refers to tomato sauce) σως
saviour σωτήρας
seven εφτά, επτά
seventeen δεκαεπτά, δεκαεφτά
sex φύλο

ship καράβι
shock σοκ
shop μαγαζί
shopping ψώνια
sign, signal σήμα
six έξι
sixteen δεκαέξι
small, little μικρός (s.),
  μικρά (pl.)
snow χιόνι
son γιος, υιός (formal Greek)
souvenir σουβενίρ
sow, i.e. female pig χοίρα
spaghetti (cooked) μακαρονάδα
Spanish Ισπανική
sport σπορ
stamps γραμματόσημα
statue άγαλμα
steak μπριζόλα
storm καταιγίδα
stranger ξένος
street οδός
stuffed (usually stuffed
  tomatoes) γεμιστά
submarine υποβρύχιο (in
  Greece it is also used to refer
  to oblong pizzas intended only
  for one. They're called
  pizza subs.)
sugar ζάχαρη
sun ήλιος
sunbathing ηλιοθεραπεία
Sunday Κυριακή (literally, the
  Lord's day)
sweater πουλόβερ
sweet γλυκό
sweets γλυκά
tank τανξ

taxi ταξί
temperature θερμοκρασία
ten δέκα
tequila τεκίλα
thank you ευχαριστώ
thermometer θερμόμετρο
thermos flask θερμό
thousand χίλια
thousands χιλιάδες
tickets εισιτήρια
time ώρα
tit bit μεζές
tomatoes ντομάτες
touch: I'm touching =
  αγγίζω
town, city πόλη
train τραίνο
truck φορτηγό
t-shirt μπλουζάκι
Tuesday Τρίτη
twelve δώδεκα
two δύο

unripe άγουρο
unsettled άστατος
untidy ακατάστατος
up πάνω, επάνω

vanilla βανίλια
vase βάζο
very πολύ
Vespa (small
  motorcycle) Βέσπα
voice φωνή

want, I θέλω
warm θερμός
Washington DC Ουάσινγκτον

watch chain καδένα
water νερό, νερά (pl.)
watermelon καρπούζι
way τρόποι
Wednesday Τετάρτη
whisky ουίσκυ
white άσπρο
why γιατί

widow χήρα
wine κρασί
wisdom σοφία
with με
xylophone ξυλόφωνο (literally,
  'voice of wood')
yoghurt γιαούρτι

Key to the exercises

Unit 1

Test yourself
1 c X **2** d xee **3** a **4** In Greek, the ' I' is pronounced as in 'if' and the stress is on the second syllable. **5** A I M N Ξ O T
6 alpha, yota, mee, nee, xee, omicron, taf

Unit 2

Exercise 1

		E	Δ	Ω
	T		E	
	A		K	
Δ	E	Ξ	I	A
Y		I		
O				

Exercise 2

a	ΔΕΚΑΟΚΤΩ	**e**	ΔΥΟ	**i**	ΔΕΚΑΕΠΤΑ
b	ΔΕΚΑ	**f**	ΕΞΙ	**j**	ΔΕΚΑΕΝΝΕΑ
c	ΔΕΚΑ	**g**	ΕΝΑ	**k**	ΔΕΚΑΕΞΙ
d	ΟΚΤΩ	**h**	ΕΝΑ	**l**	ΕΠΤΑ

Test yourself

1 c **2** b **3** b **4** b **5** Words such as decimal, decagon, December etc. are related to ΔΕΚΑ, the Greek for 'ten'. Dextrous and ambidextrous are related to ΔΕΞΙΑ. **6** Iota and ipsilon **7** Α Δ Ε Ζ Ι Μ Ν Ξ Ο Π Τ Υ Ω

Unit 3

Exercise 1

a ΕΝΑ ΚΑΦΕ **b** ΕΝΑ ΓΛΥΚΟ ΚΑΦΕ **c** ΕΝΑ ΠΟΛΥ ΓΛΥΚΟ ΚΑΦΕ

Exercise 2

1 ΔΥΟ ΚΑΦΕΔΕΣ **2** ΕΞΙ ΚΑΦΕΔΕΣ **3** ΔΕΚΑ ΚΑΦΕΔΕΣ

1 ΔΥΟ ΚΑΦΕΔΕΣ ΠΑΡΑΚΑΛΩ **2** ΕΞΙ ΚΑΦΕΔΕΣ ΠΑΡΑΚΑΛΩ
3 ΔΕΚΑ ΚΑΦΕΔΕΣ ΠΑΡΑΚΑΛΩ

Test yourself

1 1c, 2d, 3a, 4b **2** Γ Η Λ Π Ρ Σ **3** Α Γ Δ Ε Ζ Η Θ Ι Κ Λ
Μ Ν Ξ Ο Π Ρ Σ Τ Φ Ω

Unit 4

Exercise 1

1 ΟΥΖΟ	(oozo)	*ouzo*
2 ΚΡΑΣΙ	(krasi)	*wine*
3 ΝΕΡΟ	(nero)	*water*
4 ΤΕΚΙΛΑ	(tekila)	*tequila*

5 ΟΥΙΣΚΙ	(ooiski)	*whisky*
6 ΜΑΡΤΙΝΙ	(martini)	*martini*
7 ΓΑΛΑ	(wh-ala)	*milk*
8 ΛΕΜΟΝΑΔΑ	(lemonatha)	*lemonade*
9 ΠΟΡΤΟΚΑΛΑΔΑ	(portokalatha)	*orangeade*

Exercise 2

1 ΘΕΛΩ ΕΝΑ ΟΥΖΟ ΜΕ ΝΕΡΟ ΚΑΙ ΜΕΖΕ
2 ΘΕΛΟΥΜΕ ΠΑΤΑΤΕΣ ΜΕ ΚΕΦΤΕΔΑΚΙΑ
3 ΘΕΛΟΥΜΕ ΕΝΑ ΣΑΓΑΝΑΚΙ ΚΑΙ ΔΥΟ ΜΑΡΤΙΝΙ
4 ΔΥΟ ΠΑΤΑΤΕΣ ΚΑΙ ΕΝΑ ΟΚΤΑΠΟΔΙ ΠΑΡΑΚΑΛΩ
5 ΤΡΙΑ ΟΥΙΣΚΙ ΔΥΟ ΠΑΤΑΤΕΣ ΚΑΙ ΕΝΑ ΜΕΖΕ ΠΑΡΑΚΑΛΩ
6 ΘΕΛΩ ΕΝΑ ΟΥΖΟ ΜΕ ΝΕΡΟ ΚΑΙ ΜΕΖΕ
7 ΘΕΛΟΥΜΕ ΠΑΤΑΤΕΣ ΜΕ ΚΕΦΤΕΔΑΚΙΑ
8 ΘΕΛΟΥΜΕ ΣΑΓΑΝΑΚΙ ΚΑΙ ΔΥΟ ΜΑΡΤΙΝΙ
9 ΔΥΟ ΠΑΤΑΤΕΣ ΚΑΙ ΕΝΑ ΟΚΤΑΠΟΔΙ ΠΑΡΑΚΑΛΩ
10 ΤΡΙΑ ΟΥΙΣΚΙ ΔΥΟ ΠΑΤΑΤΕΣ ΚΑΙ ΕΝΑ ΜΕΖΕ ΠΑΡΑΚΑΛΩ

Exercise 3

1 ΔΕΚΑ ΜΠΟΥΚΑΛΙΑ ΜΠΥΡΑ ΠΑΡΑΚΑΛΩ
2 ΕΞΙ ΜΠΟΥΚΑΛΙΑ ΚΡΑΣΙ ΠΑΡΑΚΑΛΩ
3 ΔΥΟ ΜΠΟΥΚΑΛΙΑ ΟΥΙΣΚΙ ΠΑΡΑΚΑΛΩ
4 ΕΝΑ ΜΠΟΥΚΑΛΙ ΝΕΡΟ ΠΑΡΑΚΑΛΩ

Exercise 4

ΠΙΤΣΑΡΙΑ-ΠΙΤΣΑ; ΟΥΖΕΡΙ-ΟΥΖΟ; ΚΑΦΕΤΕΡΙΑ-ΚΑΦΕΣ;
ΜΠΥΡΑΡΙΑ-ΜΠΥΡΑ

Exercise 5

ΉΔΥΟ ΧΙΛΙΑΔΕΣ ΕΥΡΩ (thio hiliathes evro) €2000; ΕΞΙ ΧΙΛΙΑΔΕΣ
ΕΥΡΩ (exi hiliathes evro) €6000; ΔΕΚΑ ΧΙΛΙΑΔΕΣ ΕΥΡΩ (theka
hiliathes evro) €10 000; ΕΚΑΤΟ ΧΙΛΙΑΔΕΣ ΕΥΡΩ (ekato hiliathes
evro) €100 000; ΧΙΛΙΑ ΕΥΡΩ (hilia evro) €1000; ΤΡΕΙΣ ΧΙΛΙΑΔΕΣ
ΕΥΡΩ (tris hiliathes evro) €3000

Exercise 6

ΨΑΡΙ (psari) = fish   ΨΑΡΟΠΩΛΕΙΟ
ΦΡΟΥΤΑ (froota) = fruit   ΦΡΟΥΤΟΠΩΛΕΙΟ
ΤΥΡΙ (tiri) = cheese   ΤΥΡΟΠΩΛΕΙΟ
ΓΑΛΑ (wh-ala) = milk   ΓΑΛΑΚΤΟΠΩΛΕΙΟ

Test yourself
1 i Α, Δ, Ζ, Κ, Χ   **ii** Μ, Π, Φ, Ψ, Ω   **iii** Β, Θ, Ν, Ξ, Ο   **iv** Γ, Ι, Κ,
Λ, Υ   **2 i** ΤΑΒΕΡΝΑ   **ii** ΒΙΒΛΙΟ   **iii** ΨΩΜΙ ΚΑΙ ΨΑΡΙ
iv ΦΡΟΥΤΑ   **v** ΛΕΩΦΟΡΕΙΟ

Unit 5

Exercise 1

Bread	ΨΩΜΙ
Cheese	ΤΥΡΙ
Beer	ΜΠΥΡΑ
Coffee	ΚΑΦΕΣ
Sugar	ΖΑΧΑΡΗ
Retsina	ΡΕΤΣΙΝΑ
Milk	ΓΑΛΑ
Oil (to cook with)	ΛΑΔΙ
Whisky	ΟΥΙΣΚΙ
Orangeade	ΠΟΡΤΟΚΑΛΑΔΑ

Exercise 2

<u>ΣΟΥΠΕΡΜΑΡΚΕΤ:</u> ΠΟΡΤΟΚΑΛΑΔΑ, ΛΑΔΙ, ΖΑΧΑΡΗ, ΟΥΙΣΚΙ,
ΚΑΦΕΣ, ΜΠΥΡΑ, ΡΕΤΣΙΝΑ, ΨΩΜΙ
<u>ΤΥΡΟΠΩΛΕΙΟ:</u> ΤΥΡΙ; <u>ΓΑΛΑΚΤΟΠΩΛΕΙΟ:</u>   ΓΑΛΑ

Exercise 3

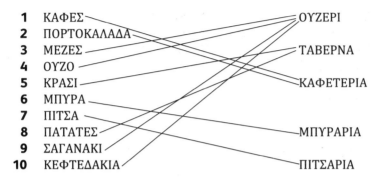

1 ΚΑΦΕΣ
2 ΠΟΡΤΟΚΑΛΑΔΑ
3 ΜΕΖΕΣ
4 ΟΥΖΟ
5 ΚΡΑΣΙ
6 ΜΠΥΡΑ
7 ΠΙΤΣΑ
8 ΠΑΤΑΤΕΣ
9 ΣΑΓΑΝΑΚΙ
10 ΚΕΦΤΕΔΑΚΙΑ

ΟΥΖΕΡΙ
ΤΑΒΕΡΝΑ
ΚΑΦΕΤΕΡΙΑ
ΜΠΥΡΑΡΙΑ
ΠΙΤΣΑΡΙΑ

Exercise 4

			Κ	Ρ	Α	Σ	Ι
			Ν	Ε	Ρ	Ο	
	Μ	Α	Ρ	Τ	Ι	Ν	Ι
	Ο	Υ	Ι	Σ	Κ	Ι	
	Τ	Ε	Κ	Ι	Λ	Α	
Λ	Ε	Μ	Ο	Ν	Α	Δ	Α
			Γ	Α	Λ	Α	

Exercise 5

ΑΥΓΑ	(av-wha)	*eggs*	ΨΩΜΙ	(psomi)	*bread*
ΓΑΛΑ	(wh-ala)	*milk*	ΑΛΑΤΙ	(alati)	*salt*
ΛΑΔΙ	(lathi)	*oil*	ΠΙΠΕΡΙ	(piperi)	*pepper*
ΤΥΡΙ	(tiri)	cheese	ΝΤΟΜΑΤΕΣ	(domates)	*tomatoes*
ΒΟΥΤΥΡΟ	(vootiro)	*butter*			

Exercise 6

AMEPIKH	ITAΛIA	EΛΛAΔA	IAΠΩNIA	KOPEA	AYΣTPAΛIA
America	Italy	Greece	Japan	Korea	Australia

Test yourself
1 Check your answers using the alphabet given below.

ΑΒΓΔΕΖΗΘΙΚΛΜΝΞΟΠΡΣΤΥΦΧΨΩ

2 Unit 1
   1 ΜΟΝΟ   **2** ΤΑΞΙ   **3** ΝΟΤΑ   **4** ΤΑΧΙ

   Unit 2
   1 ΔΕΞΙΑ   **2** ΚΑΔΕΝΑ   **3** ΔΥΟ   **4** ΤΟΞΟ

   Unit 3
   1 ΚΑΦΕ   **2** ΓΑΛΑ   **3** ΝΕΡΟ   **4** ΠΑΡΑΚΑΛΩ

   Unit 4
   1 ΟΥΖΟ   **2** ΛΕΜΟΝΑΔΑ   **3** ΛΕΩΦΟΡΕΙΟ   **4** ΜΠΑΡ

   Unit 5
   1 ΤΥΡΙ   **2** ΝΤΟΜΑΤΕΣ   **3** ΨΩΜΙ   **4** ΕΛΛΑΔΑ

Unit 6

Exercise 1

POIROT	ΠΟΥΑΡΟ
SHERLOCK HOLMES	ΣΕΡΛΟΚ ΧΟΛΜΣ
PHILIP MARLOW	ΦΙΛΙΠΠΟΣ ΜΑΡΛΟΟΥ
ELLIOT NES	ΕΛΙΟΤ ΝΕΣ
MAGNUM	ΜΑΓΚΝΟΥΜ
INSPECTOR MORSE	ΕΠΙΘΕΩΡΗΤΗΣ ΜΟΡΣ

Exercise 2

ΝΤέναλτ ΝΤάκ - Donald Duck
ΝΤειβιντ ΚΡΟΚΕΤ– Davy Crockett
ΝΤαιανα Pos - Diana Ross
ΝΤάνι ντε Βίτο - Danny de Vito

Exercise 3

ΠΙΤΣΑΡΙΑ: Πιτσαρία; ΟΥΖΕΡΙ: Ουζερί; ΚΑΦΕΤΕΡΙΑ: Καφετερία; ΜπΥΡΑΡΙΑ: Μπυραρία

Exercise 4

ΧΡΥΣΟΧΟΕΙΟ – ΧΡΥΣΟΣ – jeweller's
ΞΕΝΟΔΟΧΕΙΟ – ΔΩΜΑΤΙΟ – hotel
ΑΡΤΟΠΩΛΕΙΟ – ΨΩΜΙ – bakery
ΖΑΧΑΡΟΠΛΑΣΤΕΙΟ – ΓΛΥΚΑ – pâtisserie
ΚΑΦΕΤΕΡΙΑ – ΚΑΦΕ – cafeteria
ΕΣΤΙΑΤΟΡΙΟ – ΦΑΓΗΤΟ – restaurant
ΚΙΝΗΜΑΤΟΓΡΑΦΟΣ – ΦΙΛΜ – cinema
ΝΤΙΣΚΟΤΕΚ – ΧΟΡΟΣ – disco
ΦΑΡΜΑΚΕΙΟ – ΑΣΠΙΡΙΝΗ – chemist's
ΤΑΧΥΔΡΟΜΕΙΟ – ΓΡΑΜΜΑΤΟΣΗΜΑ – post office

Exercise 5

ΑΠΟΓΕΥΜΑΤΙΝΗ,	ΑΚΡΟΠΟΛΗ,	ΜΕΣΗΜΒΡΙΝΗ,
απογευματινή	ακρόπολη	μεσημβρινή
ΚΗΡΥΚΑΣ,	ΕΘΝΙΚΗ,	ΠΕΛΟΠΟΝΝΗΣΟΣ
κήρυκας	εθνική	πελοπόννησος

Exercise 6

5 = πέντε ευρώ   100 = εκατό ευρώ
20 = είκοσι ευρώ   200 = διακόσια ευρώ
50 = πενήντα ευρώ   500 = πεντακόσια ευρώ

Exercise 7

1–α–Α, **2**–β–Β, **3**–γ–Γ, **4**–δ–Δ, **5**–ε–Ε, **6**–ζ–Ζ, **7**–η–Η, **8**–θ–Θ, **9**–ι–Ι, **10**–κ–Κ, **11**–μ–Μ, **12**–λ–Λ

Exercise 8

It is only **Bag 2** which meets all the criteria.

Test yourself

1 μάξι μίνι κόμμα πάνω δεν λάδι γάλα κρασί ευρώ ψάρι σούπερμαρκετ βούτνρο φαρμακείο σοκολάτα γραμματόσημα

2 ΑΛΑΤΙ ΑΥΓΑ ΡΕΤΣΙΝΑ ΠΙΤΣΑ ΜΠΙΣΚΟΤΑ ΕΣΤΙΑΤΟΡΙΟ ΞΕΝΟΔΟΧΕΙΟ ΨΩΜΙ ΖΑΧΑΡΗ ΦΡΟΥΤΑ ΧΙΛΙΑ ΒΙΒΛΙΟ ΘΕΛΩ ΜΑΡΤΙΝΙ ΟΚΤΑΠΟΔΙ

Unit 7

Exercise 1

ΧΑΜΠΟΥΡΚΕΡ = hamburger; ΣΑΝΤΟΥΙΤΣ = sandwich; ΣΑΛΑΤΑ = salad; ΠΑΤΑΤΕΣ = chips; ΣΩΣ = sauce; ΚΕΤΣΑΠ = ketchup; ΜΟΥΣΤΑΡΔΑ = mustard; ΜΠΕΙΚΟΝ = bacon

Exercise 2

burger	=	χάμπουρκερ	burger	=	χάμπουρκερ
bread roll	=	ψωμάκι	bread roll	=	ψωμάκι
mustard	=	μουστάρδα	bacon	=	μπέικον
pickle	=	πίκλες	chilli	=	τσίλι
sauce	=	σως	sauce	=	σως
			onion	=	κρεμμύδι
			lettuce	=	μαρούλι
			tomatoes	=	ντομάτες

Exercise 3

1 ΨΩΜΑΚΙ **2** ΣΩΣ **3** ΜΑΡΟΥΛΙ **4** ΜΠΕΙΚΟΝ **5** ΝΤΟΜΑΤΑ

Exercise 4

1 1 **2** 1, 3, 5 **3** 2, 4 **4** 4, 5, 6

Exercise 5

ΦΙΛΕΤΑ ΨΑΡΙΟΥ, ΣΩΣ TARTAR, ΤΡΙΜΜΕΝΟ ΚΑΡΟΤΟ,
ΤΗΓΑΝΗΤΕΣ ΠΑΤΑΤΕΣ, ΑΓΓΟΥΡΙ, ΜΑΡΟΥΛΙ

Exercise 6

1 Κρέμα με Cookies **2** Κρέμα με καραμελωμένα καρύδια
3 Σοκολάτα με Choc Chips

Test yourself
1 Καρότο = Carrot, πατατάκια = chips, μπέικον = bacon, σως =
sauce, τυρί = cheese,
2 ΧΑΜΠΟΥΡΚΕΡ, ΣΩΣ, ΝΤΟΜΑΤΕΣ, ΜΑΡΟΥΛΙ, ΚΡΕΜΜΥΔΙ,
ΨΩΜΑΚΙ, ΤΣΙΛΙ, ΠΙΚΛΕΣ, ΜΟΥΣΤΑΡΔΑ, ΜΠΕΙΚΟΝ
3 ΧΑΜΠΟΥΡΚΕΡ = χάμπουρκερ, ΣΑΝΤΟΥΙΤΣ = σάντουιτς,
ΣΑΛΑΤΑ = σαλάτα, ΠΑΤΑΤΕΣ = πατάτες, ΣΩΣ = σως, ΚΕΤΣΑΠ
= κέτσαπ, ΜΟΥΣΤΑΡΔΑ = μουστάρδα, ΜΠΕΙΚΟΝ = μπέικον
4 ΜΠΕΙΚΟΝ
5 ΚΟΤΟΠΟΥΛΟ

Unit 8

Exercise 1

Monday	Tuesday	Wednesday	Thursday
ΔΕΥΤΕΡΑ	ΤΡΙΤΗ	ΤΕΤΑΡΤΗ	ΠΕΜΠΤΗ
Δευτέρα	Τρίτη	Τετάρτη	Πέμπτη

Friday	Saturday	Sunday
ΠΑΡΑΣΚΕΥΗ	ΣΑΒΒΑΤΟ	ΚΥΡΙΑΚΗ
Παρασκευή	Σάββατο	Κυριακή

Days they can go: Σάββατο and Κυριακή

Exercise 2

1 ΣΙΔΗΡΟΔΡΟΜΟΣ **2** ΛΕΩΦΟΡΕΙΟ **3** ΑΥΤΟΚΙΝΗΤΟ
4 ΠΟΥΛΜΑΝ **5** ΦΟΡΤΗΓΟ **6** ΠΟΔΗΛΑΤΟ **7** ΒΕΣΠΑ **8** ΤΖΙΠ

Exercise 3

1 ΤΖΕΙΚ ΤΟΝΤ **2** ΤΖΑΣΠΕΡ ΚΑΡΡΟΤ **3** ΤΖΕΙΜΣ
ΜΠΟΝΤ **4** ΤΖΙΛ ΑΙΡΛΑΝΤ **5** ΤΖΕΙΜΣ ΚΟΥΠΕΡ **6** ΤΖΑΚΙ
ΟΝΑΣΣΗΣ **7** ΤΖΟΝ ΓΟΥΕΙΝ

Exercise 4

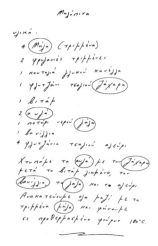

Exercise 5

1 WASHINGTON	ΟΥΑΣΙΝΓΚΤΟΝ	Ουάσινγκτον
2 LONDON	ΛΟΝΔΙΝΟ	Λονδίνο
3 ATHENS	ΑΘΗΝΑ	Αθήνα

4 MADRID   ΜΑΔΡΙΤΗ   Μαδρίτη
5 PARIS   ΠΑΡΙΣΙ   Παρίσι
6 MEXICO   ΜΕΞΙΚΟ   Μεξικό

Test yourself

Θέλω ένα φλυτζάνι τσάι και ένα φλυτζάνι καφέ μαζί με την μηλόπιτα που παράγγειλα. Στο τσάι θέλω λίγο γάλα αλλά όχι ζάχαρη και στο καφέ θέλω ζάχαρη αλλά όχι γάλα.

I want a cup of tea and a cup of coffee with the apple pie I ordered. In the tea I want a little milk but no sugar and in the coffee I want sugar and no milk.

Unit 9

Exercise 1

The only day they could have visited all the places on the tickets is Wednesday (ΤΕΤΑΡΤΗ)

Exercise 2

Γ	Α	Λ	Α	Β	Γ	Α	Ρ	Ψ	Υ	Λ	Β
Ι	Ρ	Α	Λ	Α	Λ	Μ	Α	Γ	Ω	Ρ	Α
Α	Μ	Π	Α	Ζ	Υ	Ρ	Γ	Ο	Δ	Μ	Τ
Τ	Γ	Ι	Τ	Ο	Ι	Υ	Ρ	Γ	Ι	Α	Ι
Ι	Ψ	Ρ	Ι	Τ	Θ	Ρ	Ι	Τ	Α	Ξ	Κ
Π	Λ	Ο	Υ	Σ	Α	Ε	Ε	Φ	Τ	Α	Δ
Α	Ι	Μ	Π	Α	Ρ	Γ	Λ	Δ	Ν	Υ	Σ
Π	Ο	Τ	Ο	Ψ	Μ	Ν	Ι	Ω	Ω	Μ	Α
Λ	Α	Ο	Σ	Μ	Π	Ι	Ν	Μ	Ρ	Ε	Φ
Α	Ρ	Λ	Η	Μ	Ο	Ν	Ι	Ε	Ε	Ν	Α
Δ	Ε	Ν	Μ	Π	Υ	Ρ	Α	Γ	Κ	Ι	Ν
Ι	Δ	Ε	Α	Κ	Α	Κ	Ο	Α	Α	Μ	Δ

The outlined letters are ΠΟΛΥ = *very*.

Exercise 3

αγγούρι άγγελος αγγίζω Άγγλος

Exercise 4

politics = ΠΟΛΙΤΙΚΗ
sport = ΣΠΟΡ
pullover = ΠΟΥΛΟΒΕΡ
ten = ΔΕΚΑ

Exercise 5

1	ΚΡΗΤΗ	Κρήτη
2	ΚΑΣΟΣ	Κάσος
3	ΚΑΡΠΑΘΟΣ	Κάρπαθος
4	ΧΑΛΚΗ	Χάλκη
5	ΡΟΔΟΣ	Ρόδος
6	ΣΥΜΗ	Σύμη
7	ΤΗΛΟΣ	Τηλός
8	ΝΙΣΥΡΟΣ	Νίσυρος

Exercise 6

Any combination will do here. It all depends on your own view of what constitutes a balanced meal.

Test yourself

The sequence should be: Ορεχτικά, Σαλάτες, Κύριο Πιάτο, Ζυμαρικά, Κρασιά, Αναψυκτικά

Unit 10

Exercise 1

1	χαρτί = *paper*	(ΧΑΡΤΙ)
2	ΧΑΡΤΗΣ = *map*	(χάρτης)
3	βάζο = *vase*	(ΒΑΖΟ)
4	ΒΑΖΩ = *I put*	(βάζω)
5	κριτής = *judge*	(ΚΡΙΤΗΣ)
6	ΚΡΗΤΗ = *Crete*	(κρήτη)
7	κρίνω = *I judge*	(ΚΡΙΝΩ)
8	ΚΡΙΝΟΣ = *lily*	(κρίνος)
9	φύλο = *sex* (M or F)	(ΦΥΛΟ)
10	ΦΙΛΟΣ = *friend* (M)	(φίλος)

Exercise 2

Souvenirs

1 Things you drink	**2** Things you eat	**3** Mementoes
ούζο	σοκολάτα	φωτογραφία
Ελληνικός καφές	Ελληνικό λάδι	μπλουζάκι
ρετσίνα	γλυκά	άγαλμα
πορτοκαλάδα		σημαία
μπύρα		χάρτης
		βιβλία
		εισιτήρια
		ψώνια
		δραχμές
		κασέτα
		τσάντα
		εφημερίδα

Exercise 3

1 αίθριος
2 άστατος
3 συννεφιά

4 βροχή
5 καταιγίδα
6 χιόνι
7 ομίχλη

ΠΑΡΙΣΙ, ΡΩΜΗ, ΖΥΡΙΧΗ, ΜΟΣΧΑ have a temperature higher than London.

ΛΑΜΙΑ and ΠΑΤΡΑ have the same temperature as Rome. ΜΟΣΧΑ has a temperature nearest that of London.

Acronyms

Ιησούς Χριστός, Θεού Υιός, Σωτήρ

Exercise 5

ΤΟ ΔΙΑΜΕΡΙΣΜΑ ΗΤΑΝ ΠΟΛΥ ΩΡΑΙΟ.
ΕΥΧΑΡΙΣΤΩ ΓΙΑ ΟΛΑ.
ΛΙΖΑ

Exercise 6

ΛΕΣΒΟΣ:	ΜΥΤΙΛΗΝΗ
ΧΙΟΣ:	ΧΙΟΣ
ΨΑΡΑ:	ΨΑΡΑ

Exercise 7

καράβι, αεροπλάνο, ταξί

Test yourself
1 kilo of aubergines
500 gr of potatoes
500 gr Feta cheese, grated
5 eggs
4 table spoons of flour
40 gr of Cheddar or hard cheese
½ bunch of mint chopped

Salt, Pepper

1 Heat up the over to 200° C.
2 Peel the aubergines and chips and grate them, drain them.
3 In a bowl put in all the ingredients together. Put in mint according to preferences.
4 Butter a large over-proof dish, fill it with the mix and grate hard cheese on top.
5 Bake it for about 45–60 minutes until golden.
6 Let the omelette cool, put in the fridge and use as necessary.

....

Taking it further

As with many things in life, practice makes perfect. The more that you practise pronouncing and writing Greek, the faster you will progress.

Besides working through this book, you could speed things up by practising what we call the five Cs, listed here,

- Choose a phrase book which has both Greek script and an English pronunciation guide. If there is an audio version as well, so much the better. Have a go at 'the real thing' as soon as possible, using the English version just as a check, or to help your memory. Although it may seem hard at first, it's actually quicker, because you won't rely on something which you are hoping to dispense with as soon as possible, i.e. English!
- Collect material written in Greek and English. Tourist information leaflets and maps can be particularly useful, as you can try to match up the Greek and English place names. Later on, you can try to write the name in Greek characters before checking the English equivalent. Ask for anything written in Greek from anyone with a Greek connection, or who is planning a visit to Greece or Cyprus. You can sometimes buy Greek newspapers or magazines from city centre bookstalls,

but, failing that, you might be able to persuade a friend to bring you one back from a trip. Greek newspapers can be very useful, because although the content may be advanced, you will probably be able to pick out some of the words, particularly if they are the names of people in the news. You don't want anything too upmarket – the more pictures and lurid headlines the better. Also, it's often possible to acquire menus, particularly from fast-food restaurants. Many of their dishes come straight from America, and use the same words. Impress your friends and write 'burger' in Greek! If you are lucky enough to be visiting Greece, try to work out some of the advertisements on billboards, or posters outside cinemas. Working them out can be easy and fun, as you will probably recognize many of the words. If you want to bring back memories of that Greek holiday with a suitable CD or DVD, try to pick one where the names of the tracks are given in Greek or interleaved with the English pronunciation. You will soon start to recognize some of the words if you play it often enough.

- Copy Greek words, or write them from memory. You could do this from any of the maps, leaflets or newspapers that you have acquired. If you can get hold of any books for young children, so much the better. Books for the young in any language tend to have plenty of explanatoy pictures with very simple text. You can sometimes find suitable books in secondhand bookshops. There are a few shops that sell Greek books for adults and children. Your best chance of finding one of these is to look for a bookshop in an area with a large Greek or Cypriot community.

- Chant the alphabet to yourself at odd moments. Not content with having some different letters, Greek rearranges some of the old favourites, and you will need a good sense of the order if you're not to spend frustrating hours with a Greek dictionary.

- Convert your home into a mini Greece. If you stick up common signs in appropriate places, e.g. 'open', 'closed', 'toilet' etc. you will find it easier to recognize the same letters when they occur in unfamiliar words.